Edexcel International GCSE ICT

Revision Guide

Roger Crawford

LWAYS LEARNING

PEARSON

Published by Pearson Education Limited, Edinburgh Gate, Harlow, Essex, CM20 2JE.

www.pearsonglobalschools.com

Copies of official specifications for all Edexcel qualifications may be found on the Edexcel website: www.edexcel.com

Text © Pearson Education Limited 2013
Edited by Graham Gill
Proofread by Lyn Imeson
Original design by Richard Ponsford
Typeset by Phoenix Photosetting
Original illustrations © Pearson Education Limited 2013
Indexed by Indexing Specialists (UK) Ltd.

The right of Roger Crawford to be identified as author of this work has been asserted by him in accordance with the Copyright, Designs and Patents Act 1988.

First published 2013

20 19 18 17 16 15
IMP 10 9 8 7 6 5 4 3 2

British Library Cataloguing in Publication Data
A catalogue record for this book is available from the British Library

ISBN 978 1 446 90579 1

Printed by CPI UK

Acknowledgements
The publisher would like to thank the following for their kind permission to reproduce their photographs in the book and e-book:

(Key: b-bottom; c-centre; l-left; r-right; t-top)

Alamy Images: Alex Segre 79br, Anthony Hatley 3br, Blaize Pascall 59tr, David J. Green - technology 2bl, Editorial Image, LLC 4b, kolvenbach 5br, Stephen Barnes / Technology 84br; **Fotolia.com**: Aleksandar Todorovic 79cr, goodluz 61cr, mrkob 4tl, Roman Gorielov 13tr; **Getty Images**: Bruce Bennett 56bl, Luis Alvarez 82tr, Mark Douet 78bl; **iStockphoto**: Don Nichols 81tr; **Pearson Education Ltd**: Naki Kouyioumtzis 3tr

Cover images: *Front*: **PhotoDisc**: Photodisc

All other images © Pearson Education

In some instances we have been unable to trace the owners of copyright material, and we would appreciate any information that would enable us to do so. Every effort has been made to contact copyright holders of material reproduced in this book. Any omissions will be rectified in subsequent printings if notice is given to the publishers.

Websites
Pearson Education Limited is not responsible for the content of any external internet sites. It is essential for tutors to preview each website before using it in class so as to ensure that the URL is still accurate, relevant and appropriate. We suggest that tutors bookmark useful websites and consider enabling students to access them through the school/college intranet.

A note from the publisher
In order to ensure that this resource offers high-quality support for the associated Edexcel qualification, it has been through a review process by the awarding organisation to confirm that it fully covers the teaching and learning content of the specification or part of a specification at which it is aimed, and demonstrates an appropriate balance between the development of subject skills, knowledge and understanding, in addition to preparation for assessment.

While the publishers have made every attempt to ensure that advice on the qualification and its assessment is accurate, the official specification and associated assessment guidance materials are the only authoritative source of information and should always be referred to for definitive guidance.

Edexcel examiners have not contributed to any sections in this resource relevant to examination papers for which they have responsibility.

No material from an endorsed resource will be used verbatim in any assessment set by Edexcel.

Endorsement of a resource does not mean that the resource is required to achieve this Edexcel qualification, nor does it mean that it is the only suitable material available to support the qualification, and any resource lists produced by the awarding organisation shall include this and other appropriate resources.

Contents

O —▷ Theory

▢ —▷ practicle

Introduction

Using this book to revise

This revision guide has broken the subject content down, topic by topic, to help you revise effectively and help you learn what you need to know for your International GCSE ICT examinations.

Get motivated

If you are well motivated, you are already on the road to success. If you know why you need a good grade in International GCSE ICT, you may work harder and do better. Students often find ICT interesting and enjoyable. Many jobs in ICT are well paid, and knowledge of ICT will help you in your studies in other subjects.

During the course

Preparation for the examination begins on the first day of the course:

- Try not to miss lessons. If you do, catch up quickly.

- Do all your homework to your best standard.

- Learn your work as you progress. Make sure you understand all the work you do.

- If you have problems, ask your teacher.

You can enrich your knowledge and understanding in a variety of ways:

- Read computer magazines.

- Go to local shops that sell computers and ask the sales staff about the computers they sell.

- Go on trips to computer exhibitions.

- Talk to someone who works with ICT systems and ask them about their job.

- Arrange a visit to an office or factory where ICT systems are used.

- Get your own computer and learn to use it.

Revision

You need to revise to give yourself the best possible chance of success in the examinations. You need to:

- **Start as soon as possible** – at least two months before the examination. If you leave it too late, it will feel rushed and if you come across something you don't understand there is less time for you to get to grips with it.

- **Be prepared** – identify what you need to study, practise, learn and remember.

- **Train your brain** – learn the knowledge, practise the skills and make sure you understand the key topics. It's easier to remember something if you understand it. Use this book to remind yourself of the key facts and skills, and make sure you understand them. If you need further explanation, look at the Student Book or ask your teacher.

Suggestions to help you get started

- Read the **Contents** page at the start of this book. This will give you an overview of what the book covers.

- At the start of each chapter there is a summary of what the chapter covers. Read the summaries to remind you of the subject content you need to revise and help you identify what you can do well.

- In each chapter, you will find the **key learning points** to help you revise. Diagrams and photos are included to help you understand. **Top tip** and **key fact** boxes help you identify important learning points.

- Each chapter is structured around the chapters in the **International GCSE Student Book**. This covers the content in more depth and there are more examples and case studies.

- Do the **questions at the end of each chapter**. They are in a similar style to the Edexcel International GCSE ICT examinations so they will help you practise for your examination as well as test how well you have understood each topic. There is one question with worked answers, several multiple choice questions, and questions that require more extended answers. When you answer questions in an examination you should answer in as much detail as you can in the time available. Practice this when you answer the questions.

Prepare

The key to success is preparation:

- **Manage your time effectively**. Plan when you will revise at least a week in advance and stick to your plan.

- **Choose the best environment**. Revise somewhere as quiet as possible where you will not be disturbed. Listening to music can help some to focus and revise whereas others prefer total quiet – find out what's best for you.

- **Take regular breaks**. Most people find it hard to concentrate for long periods. Take a short break every hour and an occasional longer break if you are revising all day.

- **Strike a balance**. Working all the time will not necessarily improve your performance. Overwork and worry can be as bad as not doing anything. Rest and relaxation are important to keep your body healthy and your mind fresh. It will increase your productivity when you come back to your revision.

- **Stay fit and healthy**. A headaches, broken bones and other illnesses can distract you. Avoid accidents and situations that make you ill, e.g. the day before the examination is not the right time to go sky diving! If you have unavoidable medical problems, see your doctor.

- **Get a good night's sleep**, especially the night before the exam. Have a quick look at your revision notes but don't spend all night working and worrying.

Different revision methods

Everybody learns in different ways and you need to work out what's best for you. Here are a few ways in which you can revise – you don't have to just stick to one. Sometimes a combination of several methods is the best approach:

- **Split it up**. It can be overwhelming if you try to learn everything at once. Break it down so it becomes more manageable. You could:

  - Work through this revision guide – there are twelve chapters and you could aim to revise two each week for six weeks.

- Work through the specification – ask your teacher if you need to know what this is. You can download the Edexcel International GCSE specification from: www.edexcel.com.

- Work through what you have studied lesson by lesson.

- **List the topics** that you are planning to learn and cross them off as you learn them.

- **Summarise the topic**. Write down key words and facts from what you are revising. You can use the summaries to go back over just before the exam.

- **Revise, condense and learn**. Read through all your notes and all the work you have done and, as you do this, take brief notes. Try to learn these. If there is still too much material to learn, then condense these notes again, and if necessary again.

- **Use concept maps** or **spider diagrams**. Start with a chapter title, such as 'Hardware' and break it down.

- **Improve your memory**:

  - Use **sticky notes**. You could write words and definitions on sticky notes and stick them where you will see them every day, e.g. on the bathroom mirror.

  - **Read, cover, write, check**. Read through a short unit of work several times or look at a concept map. Once you feel that you have taken it in, cover it up and then write down all the main points that you remember. Check what you have written and add anything that you forgot in a different colour. This will remind you what to focus on when you revisit the topic.

  - **Record what you need to learn**. Listening rather than reading can be more effective. If this is how you learn best then record what you want to learn and listen to it on your mobile phone, mp3 player or computer. It can also make revision more fun!

- **Do practice questions**. These will help you find out if you have learned a topic well. They also help you understand what to expect in the examinations. There are practice questions at the end of each chapter of this revision guide to help you practise. You can download papers from previous years from the Edexcel website (www.edexcel.com).

- **Revise with a friend**. You could read aloud to each other or invent tests for each other.

- **Take every opportunity to learn**. You can revise on the bus or when you are out for a walk!

Chapter 1: Hardware

What is a computer?

A computer is an electronic machine that inputs **data**, processes it under the control of a stored program, and outputs **information**. While the data is being processed, data can be retrieved from or saved on backing storage.

Data is raw, unprocessed information. Information is data that people understand. In order to understand data, you may have to interpret it:

The number 30112012 is data that can be interpreted as:

- A date 30/11/2012

- A sum of money $301,120.12

The interpreted data, that is the date or the sum of money, is the information.

- **Input** – data is entered into the computer.

- **Process** – a computer is controlled by a **program**, that is, a sequence of instructions. It processes the input data automatically following these instructions.

- **Store** – the program and data are stored, e.g. on a hard disk, for later retrieval.

- **Output** – the computer communicates to the user, e.g. it displays graphics on the screen.

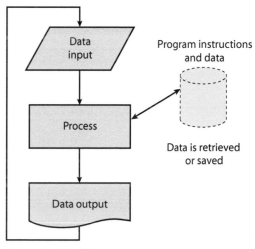

Figure 1.1 *Flow of data*

Types of computer

Computers can be:

- **PCs (personal computers)** – a microcomputer for individual use.
- **Mainframe computers** – large computer, with huge processing power.
- **Minicomputers** – smaller version of a mainframe.
- **Supercomputers** – very large mainframe.

Different types of PC

- **Desktop** – has these basic components: monitor, keyboard, system unit and mouse.
- **Laptop** – a portable computer slightly larger than A4 size.
- **Tablet** (or **pad**) – a very small portable computer with a touch-sensitive screen and no keyboard.
- **Notebook** – a small laptop computer.
- **Netbook** – very small laptop optimised for Internet and email access.
- **Hand-held** computer, e.g. smart phone – fits into one hand and has a touch-sensitive screen. Can be temporarily attached to a keyboard.
- **Games console** – a PC designed for playing games, e.g. Xbox. Has these features:
  - Graphics displayed very quickly
  - Large hard disk
  - Game controller, e.g. joysticks, buttons
  - Internet connection for online games.
- **Embedded computer** – designed for and built into equipment to perform specialised functions, e.g. a single microchip that controls a DVD player.

Processors

A **processor** or microprocessor is built into a microchip that also has memory and other components built into it. The microchip itself is often referred to as the 'processor'. If there is more than one processor built into the microchip, then the microchip is referred to as the 'processor' and processors built into it are referred to as '**cores**'.

An important feature of a processor is the speed at which it processes instructions. If you have more and faster cores, with a larger on-board cache, applications will run more quickly.

Here is a microprocessor description: Intel Core 2 Duo E8600 Processor (3.33GHz, 1333MHz FSB, 6MB cache). This has two cores and their speed is 3.33GHz. The **front side bus** (FSB) transfers data between the processor and memory at a speed of 1333MHz. A 6MB **cache** of RAM memory is built into the microprocessor.

Figure 1.2 *An Intel Core 2 Duo microprocessor*

The processor you need depends on what you are going to do. For occasional word processing and email, an Intel Pentium Dual Core processor might be sufficient but for playing online multimedia games a faster Intel Pentium Quad Core processor is needed.

Input and output devices

- The **peripheral** devices attached to a computer system are for input, output or storage.
- An **input** device is for putting in data to the computer.
- An **output** device displays information from the computer.

Input device	Output device
Keyboard	Monitor
Mouse	Printer
Scanner	Speakers and headphones

Input devices

Keyboards

A **QWERTY keyboard** is used with most PCs and laptops. To use a keyboard efficiently, you need to know the layout and be able to touch-type. **Numeric keyboards** only have keys to input numbers and special characters. An example of a numeric keypad is an automated teller machine (ATM), also known as a cashpoint.

Figure 1.3 *An automated teller machine (ATM) or cashpoint showing the numeric keypad*

Pointing devices

Compared with a keyboard, pointing devices make it easier to point and click but are harder to use to input text.

- **Mouse** – an optical mouse detects movement using light but some do this using a small rubber ball.
- **Joystick** – a lever that gives you similar control to a mouse. Joysticks are built into game consoles, which are mainly used for input but may have limited output, e.g. they vibrate.
- **Tracker ball** – like an upside-down ball mouse with the ball on the top. Move the ball with your thumb.
- **Trackpad** – a pad below the space bar on a laptop. Move your fingers across its surface and the pointer moves on the screen.
- **Graphics tablet** – a flat rectangular pad 15 to 76 cm (6 to 30 inches) wide. Move a stylus along its surface to produce line drawings. Mainly used for computer-aided design.

Figure 1.4 *Graphics tablet and puck being used to trace a drawing*

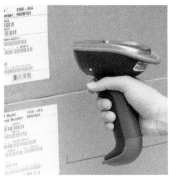

Figure 1.5 *A bar code scanner*

Scanners

A scanner converts printed images on paper into electronic form:

- **Hand-held scanner** – reads the image while being dragged over it.

- **Flatbed scanner** – the image is laid flat on the scanner's surface.

- **Sheet-fed scanner** – reads the image as the paper goes through the sheet feeder.

Scanners may read only particular types of image, e.g. a **bar code scanner**.

Optical Mark Recognition (OMR)

An **OMR** reader recognises a mark made on paper so there is no need to type in the data. The mark's position determines its meaning. Marks must be very clear, or they may not be recognised.

Optical Character Recognition (OCR)

OCR is used to input printed or handwritten characters without typing in the data. The characters are converted to text that can be word processed. This text needs to be checked carefully as character recognition is not always accurate.

Magnetic ink character recognition (MICR)

MICR is used to input specially shaped characters printed in magnetic ink. Forms can be pre-printed with data which can be read by a computer, but printing in magnetic ink is more expensive.

OCR vs MICR

- OCR and MICR both read printed characters.

- OCR uses reflected light while MICR uses magnetic field patterns.

- OCR recognises handwriting and different types of printed text but MICR only recognises specially shaped characters.

TOP TIP ✓

When you describe the difference between two technologies, each point you make should mention both technologies.

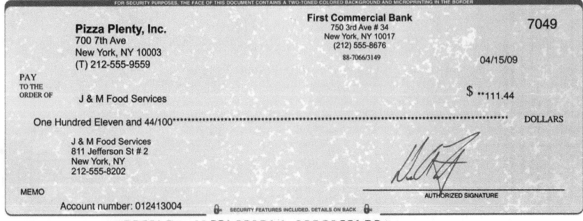

Figure 1.6 *MICR uses uniquely shaped characters printed in magnetic ink*

Magnetic stripe cards

- Information is stored on a **magnetic stripe** on a plastic card. The data recorded on the magnetic stripe can be input directly into a computer. Stripe cards can be used to control access. A disadvantage of stripe cards is that the data may be affected by electromagnetic radiation and data can also be copied or edited.

Smart cards

- A **smart card** is a plastic card with a microprocessor chip embedded in it.
- Bank and credit cards are usually smart cards, i.e. **Chip and PIN** (personal identification number) cards.
- They are used to pay for goods in shops and to withdraw cash at cashpoints. Cashpoints are specialised computer terminals with a small screen, numeric keyboard and smart card reader.
- Oyster® cards are smart cards in widespread use in London to pay for travel. They are preloaded with cash credits online.
- Smart cards can also be affected by electronic radiation and can be copied or edited but they are generally more secure than data recorded on a magnetic stripe.

Digital cameras, digital video cameras and webcams

- A **digital camera** stores pictures on a memory card. These can be transferred to a computer or TV. Digital cameras have a small LCD screen or traditional viewfinder. The camera forms pictures from a mass of very small dots of different colours. Picture quality is related to the density of the dots.
- A **digital video camera** or camcorder records moving images with sound. Recordings can be saved on a memory card or built-in hard disk, and input to a computer.
- A **webcam** is a digital video camera used to view a remote location over the Internet. This may be for security purposes, interest or communication. Recordings can be made. Simple webcams have a fixed position but some webcams allow the user to turn them.

Digital photos and videos can be:

- Saved on a computer, so backup is easier and more reliable.
- Sent by email.
- Displayed on a wide variety of devices, such as smartphones and TV screens.
- Broadcast over the Internet, e.g. on-demand TV programmes.

Disadvantages:

- Users store more photos and longer videos so more backing storage is needed.
- High-quality photos and videos can be very large files. Sent by email or broadcast over the Internet they use more bandwidth and slow the network.

Biometric scanners

A **biometric scanner** reads a person's unique physical characteristics to identify them, e.g. face recognition. Biometric scanners can be used to control entry to buildings and used in place of car keys. Although identification is not entirely accurate, the use of biometric scanners minimises the risk of fraud and theft.

Figure 1.7 *A biometric scanner using fingerprints*

Sensors

- **Sensors** are used to input environmental data.

- Examples of uses include recording light intensity, pressure and temperature.

- Each sensor only detects one type of data.

- Sensors usually produce a low analogue voltage which must be converted to a digital signal for the computer using an ADC (analogue-to-digital converter).

Sensors are used extensively for data logging and control as data can be continuously and reliably recorded in a form that can be processed by a computer, e.g. in weather stations and robotics. They can be placed in dangerous locations where people would be hurt and can record data that people do not sense accurately, e.g. humidity. Data can be collected frequently over networks from sensors in remote locations.

Audio input devices and technologies

Computer input of sound has a variety of uses:

- A **touch-tone telephone** makes a different beep depending on the button pressed. On the other end of the line, a computer inputs the beep and determines which button has been pressed. You may then listen to a voice response from the computer.

- A **microphone** is used to input sound.

- **Voice recognition** software enables the computer to know who is talking but not what has been said.

- **Speech recognition** is often used for **voice command systems**. The speaker is identified and spoken words recognised as commands.

- **Natural language processing** uses speech recognition to interpret natural language, e.g. spoken English. You could use natural language processing to dictate a letter or give instructions to a computer.

Advantages of audio input:

- People speak to the computer and do not need to learn to operate a keyboard.

Disadvantages:

- Voice and speech recognition software has to be trained to recognise each person's speech. This can be a lengthy process.

- Voice and speech recognition is not accurate because people pronounce words differently.

Remote control

Remote controls are used to control TVs and garage doors and inaccessible or hidden devices. However, if the handset is lost or damaged, the device may not be useable.

Figure 1.8 The LEDs built into a remote handset

A remote control handset will often have two LEDs. One LED is the infrared transmitter and the light from this is invisible. The other emits a visible light to reassure the user that the remote control is working.

The remote control technology used in the home is usually infrared. The **transmitter** built into the handset sends out a coded pulse of infrared light when a button is pressed. A transmitter is often a light-emitting diode (LED). A **receiver** built into the device being controlled inputs the code and passes it to a microprocessor that carries out the command.

Output devices

Monitors

- Monitors or visual display units (VDUs) come in different styles with different screen resolutions, colour quality and clarity.

- LCD (liquid crystal display) monitors have flat screens and are more compact than CRT (cathode ray tube) monitors. They consume less power than CRTs.

- A monitor screen is made up of many dots (**pixels** or picture elements). The dots are so tiny you do not usually see them. A screen has a **resolution** of 1280 by 1024 if there are 1280 dots across the screen, and 1024 from top to bottom. Higher quality screens display more dots.

- The **graphics card** (or **video card)** is housed in the system unit and controls the screen display. Higher quality cards have more colours and produce clearer graphics more quickly.

Touch screen

A touch screen is used for output and input. You touch the screen to control the computer. Touch screens are mainly used with tablets and smartphones. There is no need for a keyboard but inputting text is slower.

Multimedia projector

A **multimedia projector** projects the image displayed on a computer screen onto a larger, separate screen, which can be seen more clearly by a large audience. **Interactive whiteboards** are large, touch-sensitive panels used as screens for multimedia projectors. This technology is used in school classrooms and at home to watch movies and play computer games.

Printers

Printed output is called **printout** or **hard copy.**

> - **An impact printer** strikes through an inked ribbon onto paper.
> - A **non-impact printer** uses a non-striking method to form the image on the paper.

- Some **dot-matrix printers** are impact printers with a print head that is a matrix of steel pins. The pins strike a carbon ribbon making patterns of dots on the paper.

- **Inkjet printers** spray tiny dots of ink onto the paper. Inkjet printers are non-impact dot matrix printers and are quieter. They produce high-quality output in monochrome or colour.

Figure 1.9 *Enlarged dot-matrix printing produced by an inkjet printer showing how the dots form characters*

- **Laser printers** are widely used but are more expensive to buy than inkjet printers. Quality is excellent and they print quickly in monochrome or colour.

- **Thermal printers** use heated wires to mark dots on the surface of a heat-sensitive paper.

Printers use different types of paper, for example:

- **Single sheets** of A4 paper.

- **Continuous paper** is perforated and can be easily separated into single pages.

- **Pre-printed stationery** has information on the paper before computer printing. For example, the name and address of the company.

Print quality

- Printers use very small dots to produce text and pictures. A measure of print quality is the **dpi** (number of **dots per inch).** The higher the dpi, the better the print quality.

Photo-printers

- **Photo-printers** are used to print digital photographs. A digital camera is connected to the printer or the camera's memory card is read in the printer. Pictures can be printed without using a computer.

Advantages of printers:

- A printout is useful if no computer is available.

Disadvantages:

- Printing is slow and expensive compared with electronic communications.
- Paper is bulky and deteriorates in storage.
- Printed materials are more difficult to access and distribute, e.g. digital photos can be emailed and viewed on a multimedia projector.

Plotters

- A **plotter** draws lines on paper using coloured pens. A **flatbed** plotter holds the paper still while the pens move. Other plotters move the pens from left to right while the paper moves forwards and backwards. An **upright** plotter uses very long sheets of paper. Plotters are used in **computer-aided design.** Plotters are usually more expensive to buy and slower than printers, but much larger sheets can be printed.

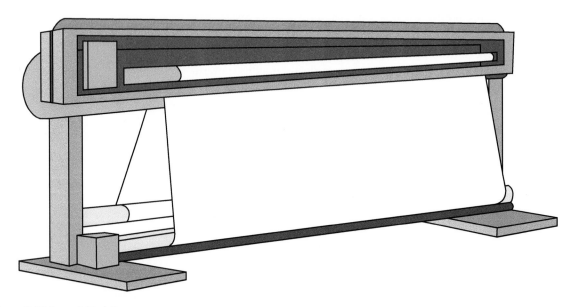

Figure 1.10 *An upright plotter*

Multi-function devices (MFD)

- **MFDs** combine a printer, scanner and communications link to function as a printer, scanner, photocopier or fax machine. MFDs are much less expensive to buy than all the individual devices and use less space on the desktop. It is cost effective to replace them more frequently with modern technology. However, if part of the device is faulty, all the functions may be unavailable. If one function is being used, then the other functions are unavailable for other users.

Speakers

Many computers have **speakers**. **Headphones** are two small speakers built into a headset. Sound is needed, for example, to play music and for speech synthesis.

Sound cards

A **sound card** controls all input and output of audio. Audio input through a microphone and output through speakers are usually analogue and the sound card handles their conversion into digital signals processed by the computer. It also handles digital audio input, e.g. from multimedia applications.

Sound cards have features such as:

- **Polyphony** – plays more than one sound or voice independently at the same time.

- Output through one or more sound **channels,** e.g. mono, stereo (2 channels), or quadraphonic (4 channels).

- Surround sound or 3D audio.

- Improves the clarity of compressed audio files, e.g. mp3.

- Built-in memory for faster sound processing.

- USB, optical and other ports to connect to DVD recorders and other devices.

- MIDI (Musical Instrument Digital Interface) to connect to electronic instruments.

> Sound cards are built into or plugged into the motherboard of a PC, or can be external devices that plug into a USB port.

Actuators

In control applications, computers make events happen using **actuators**, e.g. heaters and motors. A buzzer is an actuator that, for example, warns when the microwave has cooked our dinner. Actuators can perform physical tasks such as controlling a robot or operating a digger. This can be dangerous for people if their presence is not detected by the computer.

Worked Example

A desktop PC is used for office work at an Estate Agent.

a) State one input device needed and explain why it is needed.

b) State one output device needed and explain why it is needed.

c) The office is cramped and the manager purchases an MFD to replace the photocopier.

    i. Name three other hardware devices an MFD replaces.

    ii. State one advantage and one disadvantage of purchasing the MFD.

TOP TIP ✔

Relate your answers to the context, i.e. the Estate Agent.

Answers

a) There are several correct answers, e.g. a digital camera is used to take digital pictures of houses for sale to upload to the Estate Agent's website.

b) There are several correct answers, e.g. a colour printer is used to print details of houses for sale to be given to customers.

c)   i. Printer; scanner; fax machine.

    ii. There are several correct answers. For example: Advantage: MFDs are more compact than the individual devices replaced. Disadvantage: If the MFD breaks down this has more impact on office work than if an individual device is not working.

Exam-Style Questions

1. A printer is a type of:

    A   processor

    B   input device

    C   software

    D   output device   *(1 mark)*

2. Which of these devices is **not** used to control a screen pointer?

    A   a mouse

    B   a trackpad

    C   a webcam

    D   a joystick   *(1 mark)*

3. Which type of computer is the most portable?

    A   supercomputer

    B   desktop

    C   mainframe

    D   tablet   *(1 mark)*

4. A biometric scanner controls access to a secure warehouse. One advantage is:

    A   No one can get into the warehouse

    B   No need to carry a swipe card

    C   Biometric scanners always recognise banned users

    D   Identity theft is difficult   *(1 mark)*

5. Other than the keyboard, name an input device you would use to:

    a) Select from a menu.   *(1 mark)*

    b) Convert a page of printed text to a file that can be word processed.   *(1 mark)*

6. State whether each of the following is used for input or output or both. Explain your answers.

    a) Printer   *(2 marks)*

    b) Game console   *(2 marks)*

7. Smart phones have touch screens.

    a) Explain why a smart phone has a touch screen.   *(1 mark)*

    b) State **two** uses of a smart phone other than making phone calls.   *(2 marks)*

    c) Explain why some smart phones connect to external keyboards.   *(1 mark)*

8. The resolution of a monitor screen is changed from 1280x1024 to 800x600. State one change you would see on the screen display.   *(1 mark)*

9. A student owns a desktop computer and a tablet computer. Explain why.   *(3 marks)*

Chapter 2: Backing storage and memory

You need to know:

- The size of memory, backing storage and files are measured in bytes:

  1 kilobyte = 1024 bytes

  1 megabyte = 1024 kilobytes

  1 gigabyte = 1024 megabytes

  1 terabyte = 1024 gigabytes.

- **RAM** is main memory (random-access memory). Data and programs in main memory are lost when the computer is turned off.
- **ROM** (read-only memory) stores data permanently.
- **Backing storage** saves your data when the computer is turned off.
- **Backing storage media** includes: hard disks, CDs, DVDs, magnetic tapes, memory cards and memory sticks.
- **Flash memory** is used for memory cards and memory sticks.
- **Backups** are copies of files and help prevent data loss.

Bits and bytes

Bit (**bi**nary dig**it**) patterns in memory and on **backing storage** represent, e.g. characters, numbers, graphics and sounds. A **byte** stores 8 bits, each of which can be either 1 or 0. Different computers access one, two, four or more bytes of data at a time. If a computer can read/write four bytes at once, this is 32-bit computing.

Memory

A computer's main memory is RAM and ROM.

Comparison of RAM and ROM	
RAM	**ROM**
Can be written to and read from.	Can only read from.
Holds programs being run and data being processed.	Stores programs and data permanently.
Volatile – it is cleared when the computer is switched off.	**Non-volatile** – it retains what is stored when the computer is turned off.
RAM microchips are supplied as a module (several chips on a small board) plugged into the motherboard.	ROM microchips are installed in the motherboard.

Flash memory in the computer

Flash memory is a type of ROM that can be written to and read from and is used for the **BIOS (basic input/output system)** in PCs. This makes sure the computer starts up as it should and that all the parts of the computer work together.

Backing storage devices and media

Backing storage saves your files when the computer is turned off.

> • Backing storage **media** is a DVD, for example.
>
> • A backing storage **device** is the DVD drive used to read the DVD, for example.

Flash memory

Memory sticks store up to 32 GB of data and plug into the USB port on a computer. Memory sticks are sometimes called USB sticks, pen drives and USB pens. They are:

- Inexpensive

- Small

- Lightweight

- A convenient way of moving data from one computer to another.

Read/write head

Figure 2.1 *The inside of fixed hard disk with moveable heads*

Memory cards store up to 256 GB of data. There are many types, including SD (Secure Digital) and mini and micro SD. They are used in, e.g. digital cameras and mobile phones.

Hard disks

A magnetic **hard disk** stores 500 GB of data or more. On each surface, the data is stored in concentric tracks and there is a **read/write head** that moves in/out to the track where the data is saved.

Types of hard disk:

- **Internal** hard disks are built into computers.

- **External** hard disks are portable and often connected to a computer by USB.

Optical disks

CDs, DVDs, HD DVD and Blu-ray are **optical disks** and are read and written by a laser.

TOP TIP ✓

Do not confuse the hard disk and RAM memory. The hard disk stores your work when the computer is switched off whereas RAM is cleared.

CDs (Compact disks)

A CD stores around 700 MB. Data read/write is slower than a hard disk. CDs are easily damaged but inexpensive.

DVDs (Digital versatile disks)

A single-sided, single-layer DVD stores around 4.7 GB. A dual-layer, two-sided DVD stores 18 GB. Data read/write is slower than a hard disk.

There are many different types of CD and DVD, for example:

- Data can be read from but not written to **CD-ROM** and **DVD-ROM.** Often used for movies.

- **CD-RW and DVD-RW** can be rewritten repeatedly up to 1000 times.

Compatibility problems

Many drives cannot read all types of CD and DVD, e.g. some CD players do not play MP3 files.

- **DVD-RAM** may be sealed in a cartridge and can be rewritten more than 100 000 times. Used to store data for up to 30 years.

- **HD DVD** is similar to a DVD but with sufficient capacity for high definition movies.

- A dual-layer **Blu-ray** disk can store 50 GB. Used for high-definition movies.

Figure 2.2 *An external hard drive*

Magnetic tapes

A magnetic tape stores a great quantity of data but read/write is slow because it is **serial access** – the tape is read from the beginning to find the data needed. **Magnetic tape cartridges** are often used for backup.

Backup

A **backup** is a copy of a file. Backup a file each time you edit it (e.g. save it on the internal hard disk in your PC and save a backup on an external hard disk), and backup all your files every month (e.g. to DVDs).

> Make regular backups so you have a recent copy in case your work is corrupted or lost, e.g. due to a hard drive crash.

Keep backups of your personal files:

- Next to the computer for convenient use.

- In a fireproof safe nearby in case the building burns down.

- In another location far away in case local backups are all destroyed.

Backups of large ICT systems with networked hard disks:

- Usually done every day automatically over the network.

- Can be saved anywhere in the world.

- Backing storage devices can be enclosed in fireproof, waterproof and bombproof containers.

- Software keeps track of when backups were taken and where they are stored.

- When a file is lost and needs to be recovered, the backup software searches for the most up-to-date version.

TOP TIP ✓

You need to make backups of your own work and do this systematically. Apply the theory to your practice.

Worked Example

1. Give **one** reason why a backup is taken.

2. Name **two** types of backing storage media used for backup.

3. Describe **three** places you would store a backups.

Answers

1. So you have a copy in case your work is corrupted or lost.

2. Magnetic tape cartridge, external hard disk.

3. In an accessible location near to the computer, in a fireproof safe in the same building, in another city.

1. Which of these provides the largest storage capacity?

    A   5 GB

    B   128 MB

    C   1 TB

    D   20Kb   *(1 mark)*

2. A memory stick stores 2 GB of data. How many CDs are needed to store the same data?

    A   4

    B   3

    C   6

    D   2   *(1 mark)*

3. A DVD is an example of:

    A   a hard disk

    B   RAM

    C   an optical disk

    D   flash memory   *(1 mark)*

4. Which of the following is storage media?

    A   CD

    B   DVD drive

    C   a kilobyte

    D   printer   *(1 mark)*

5. Preparing backup storage media so that it can store your files is known as:

    A   formatting

    B   optical storage

    C   backup

    D   storage capacity   *(1 mark)*

6. Describe two differences between RAM and ROM.   *(2 marks)*

7. Describe two differences between a USB memory stick and a hard disk. *(2 marks)*

TOP TIP

When you are asked to describe the differences between two technologies, each point you make should mention both technologies.

8. Many people think main memory and the hard disk are the same. Describe how they are similar, and how they are different.   *(4 marks)*

TOP TIP

Many people wrongly use the term 'memory' when referring to both the hard disk and main memory. Try to avoid such misconceptions and demonstrate you understand why they arise.

9. Why is a hard disk with fixed read/write heads likely to access data faster than a hard disk with moveable heads?   *(1 mark)*

Chapter 3: Software

Applications software

Office productivity software, presentation software and project management software

Office productivity software helps you do office tasks and includes:

- **Word processing** software, e.g. Microsoft Word. Helps you prepare documents that include text and pictures. You can edit the text, change the font and size, check your spelling and grammar, print, and save and retrieve documents.

- **Desktop publishing (DTP)** software, e.g. Microsoft Publisher. Handles page layout better than word processing software.

- **Spreadsheet** software, e.g. Microsoft Excel. Performs calculations on tables of numbers arranged in rows and columns with related headings and charts. If a number is changed, the spreadsheet automatically recalculates.

- **Database** software, e.g. Microsoft Access. Used to maintain records, e.g. a library stores the name, address and membership number of borrowers. A database can search these records and print reports.

- **Presentation** software, e.g. Microsoft PowerPoint, helps you prepare and give a multimedia presentation to an audience. This could include: slides with text, graphics, hyperlinks and notes for the speaker.

- **Project management** software, e.g. Microsoft Project, is used to track the timelines of all the tasks that have to be done to complete a project, e.g. when constructing a building. Timelines are displayed in a Gantt chart.

> **Integrated** software has several applications bundled into one package (e.g. Microsoft Office). Data is transferred more easily between the different applications, e.g. an Excel spreadsheet can be copied into a Word document.

Web browser software, communications software and web authoring software

- Using **web browser** software, e.g. Mozilla Firefox, you can access **websites** by entering their web address or **URL (uniform resource locator)** or clicking on **hyperlinks**.

- Using a **search engine**, e.g. Google, you can search the Web by entering keywords.

- **Email** is accessed using:

  - an email client running on your own computer, e.g. Microsoft Outlook.

  - webmail, that is, email accessed using a web browser.

- **Web authoring** software, e.g. Adobe Dreamweaver, is used to create and update websites. A website is a structured collection of web pages written in **HTML (Hypertext Markup Language)**.

Image and sound editing software

- **Graphics** software, e.g. Adobe Photoshop, is used to create and retouch, crop and resize images.

- **Video editing** software, e.g. Microsoft Movie Maker, is used to edit videos imported from digital cameras and camcorders. You can insert titles, transitions, voiceovers and sound effects, and save the video in different formats, e.g. mp4.

- **Audio editing** software, e.g. Audacity, is used to create and edit music and sounds. You can record live music and input digital sound files, insert voiceovers, and change pitch and tempo.

Control software

Control software is used to monitor and control external devices, e.g. robots, and ICT systems, for purposes such as air conditioning in large buildings. Computers do this using sensors and actuators. Sensors are devices that can measure variables such as pressure, temperature and humidity. Actuators make changes under the control of the computer – some examples are motors, pumps and heaters.

Educational software

- A wide range of **educational** software supports teaching and learning, e.g. StarFrench helps you learn French, and SpexClassic helps with teaching design and technology.

Operating System (OS) software

What is an operating system?

The **operating system (OS)** controls the computer so that applications software can run. An OS does many tasks including:

- Control of all input and output.

- Error handling, e.g. if the printer is out of paper the OS displays a message on the screen.

- Resource allocation. More than one application could be running on the computer and these may want to use the same resource (e.g. the processor). If only one processor is being used, the OS interleaves the different applications; if there are several cores, the OS decides which are used.

- Providing a user interface so that you can interact with the computer.

- File handling. File-handling software, e.g. Windows Explorer, enables you to format disks, create new files and folders, and rename, save, open, delete and copy them.

An OS also includes **system software tools** (or **utility** programs) to help you maintain your computer, e.g. a **disk defragmenter**. A file saved on a hard disk can become fragmented with different parts saved in different places. A disk defragmenter will reassemble all the different parts to speed up access.

User interfaces

An OS can have a:

- **Command-line** user interface. This can be difficult to use because you have to remember the exact instructions (format and syntax) to use.

- **Menu-driven** user interface. You choose an option from a menu. This is easier to use because you don't have to remember the exact instruction.

- **Graphical user interface (GUI)**, e.g. Windows. GUIs are more user-friendly. You do not have to remember complex instructions or menu options.

Figure 3.1 *A command-line user interface*

Graphical User Interface (GUI)

A GUI has:

- **Windows, icons and menus**. You select icons and menu options by pointing and clicking.

- **Toolbars**, e.g. in Windows 7, in the Computer window, the toolbar includes the File, Edit and View menus. In the View menu, if you point at Sort by, a **sub-menu** appears.

- **Scrollbars** enable you to look at content not currently shown on screen.

- **Dialog boxes** convey messages to you and invite a response.

Figure 3.2 *A graphical user interface (GUI)*

Using a mouse with a GUI (e.g. Windows), you can:

- **Open** (activate) a process, e.g. by pointing at an icon and double-clicking the left-hand mouse button.

- **Move** an icon, e.g.by pointing at an icon, holding down the left button, dragging it to the required location and releasing the button.

- **Close** a process, e.g. by selecting Exit in the File menu.

A GUI (e.g. Windows) can be **customised**:

- **Window size and position** can be adjusted, e.g. drag the bottom right-hand corner of a window to change its size and drag the title bar to move it around the screen. The **minimize** button removes the window from the screen but does not close it; the **maximize** button makes the window occupy the whole screen.

- **Mouse settings**, **icon size** and **sound volume** can be adjusted.

- Desktop themes, colours, contrast and backgrounds can be personalised.

File handling

- A **filename** has two parts: the **name** identifies the file and the **extension** identifies the type of file, e.g. **study.xls** has the name 'study' and the extension 'xls' which means it is an Excel spreadsheet.

- Files are grouped into **folders.** The route to a file is called its **path,** e.g. C:\Users\Documents\chapter3. doc. This means that on the hard disk C: in the **folder** 'Users', in the **sub-folder** 'Documents' there is a file named 'chapter3' which is a word processor file.

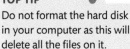

TOP TIP

Do not format the hard disk in your computer as this will delete all the files on it.

- In Windows Explorer, to move or copy a file, select the file, drag it over another folder and drop it. To delete a file, right-click on the filename and select Delete.

- You can set the properties of a file, e.g. read-only. A read-only file can only be opened but cannot be altered.

Software licensing

Software is **copyrighted**. It is illegal to use it without a **software licence**. Types of license are:

- **Licensed software.** Purchasers buy the right to use it.

- **Public domain** software is free and has no restrictions on its use but you might not be given the source code.

- **Open source.** Licences are free and you have access to the source code and are allowed to modify it.

- **Shareware** is licensed software that is initially free to try out. However, you must pay for a licence if you decide to make regular use of it.

- **Creative Commons** licences help software producers communicate the rights they keep for themselves and the rights they give to others.

Worked Example

Steven has application software installed on his computer.

a)   Name **three** types of application software.

b)   Name **one** type of software that must be installed to run the applications.

c)   Steven buys a computer game that includes a software licence. Explain why Steven needs a software licence.

d)   Access to the software on Steven's hard disk becomes very slow. What could Steven do to speed up access?

Answers

a)   Any reasonable answer, e.g. word processor, database, spreadsheet, email.

b)   Operating system.

c)   It would be illegal to play the game without a license that allows this. The license will tell Steven what use he can make of the software, e.g. he can only install it on one computer and make one back up.

d)   Any reasonable answer, e.g. run disk defragmenter.

1. What type of software is used to prepare a talk to be given to a large audience?
   - A Spreadsheet
   - B Desk Top Publishing
   - C Email
   - D Presentation *(1 mark)*

2. You receive an email from one friend and send it to another friend. This is known as:
   - A deleting
   - B attaching
   - C forwarding
   - D replying. *(1 mark)*

3. Which of the following is **not** applications software:
   - A operating system
   - B word processing
   - C video editing
   - D web authoring *(1 mark)*

4. Which of the following is false?
   - A A folder may contain sub-folders.
   - B A folder may contain files.
   - C mybudget.xls is a spreadsheet file.
   - D A file contains folders. *(1 mark)*

5. Which of the following would it be illegal to copy and give to a friend?
   - A Software with a Creative Commons Attribution licence
   - B Public domain software
   - C licensed software
   - D open source software *(1 mark)*

6. Describe **two** tasks that could be done using audio editing software. *(2 marks)*

7. a) Name one example of an integrated software package. *(1 mark)*
   b) Name **two** different applications integrated within the package. *(2 marks)*

8. Describe how you would format a USB memory stick using a GUI. *(4 marks)*

TOP TIP

When you are asked to describe a process, make sure each step in the process is in the right order and clearly described.

9. a) Describe **two** tasks carried out by the operating system. *(2 marks)*
   b) Describe what the operating system would do if five programs wanted to use at the same time a processor with four cores. *(1 mark)*

Chapter 3: Software

Chapter 4: Word processing and desktop publishing

> **You need to know:**
>
> You need to know how to use software for **word processing**, e.g. Microsoft Word, and **DTP (desktop publishing)**, e.g. Microsoft Publisher. This chapter reminds you which features of this software you should be able to use. However, run the software and make sure you can use it.
>
> A **word processor** has many features to help you to prepare letters and other documents:
>
> - The **GUI** has toolbars and buttons that help you use the features.
> - You can **open**, **close**, **save** and **print** documents.
> - There are many **editing features**.
> - You can check your written **language**, spelling and grammar using tools.
> - **Formatting** determines the appearance of a document, including character and paragraph formatting.
> - There are many **page layout** features.
> - **Tables** can be inserted.
> - **Templates** can be used to create new documents with the same format.
> - **Mail merge** allows you to produce personalised documents quickly.
> - **Graphics** can be inserted into a document and edited.
> - **Drawing tools** include callouts and 3-D effects.
> - A complex illustration can be put together using several smaller **clip art** or **shape** objects.
>
> **Desktop publishing (DTP)** software is used to produce leaflets and newspapers:
>
> - There are many features in common with word processing but **page layout** is emphasised.
> - Information is inserted in **frames** and an important feature is **text flow** between frames.

Word processing

A **word processor** is used to prepare letters and other documents, e.g. Microsoft Word 2010, which is used for the examples in this chapter. It has many features found in most word processors.

The GUI

The GUI has features typical of many word processors:

- The **insertion point** is a flashing vertical line which shows where text appears when you type on the keyboard.

- The **I-beam** or mouse pointer allows you to move the insertion point to a specific position in a document by clicking on the left mouse button.

- **Vertical scrollbars** allow you to scroll up or down.

- **Horizontal scrollbars** allow you to scroll left or right.

- **Page buttons** allow you to move up or down a document a page at a time.

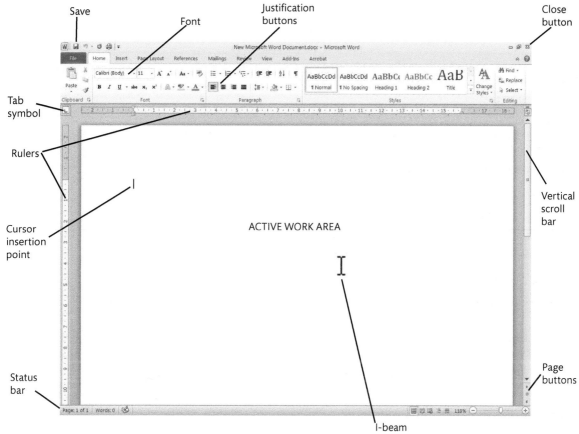

Figure 4.1 *The Microsoft Word GUI*

Open and Close

To create a new document, open Word, or if Word is open, click on the **File** tab and select **New**. To open a document you have previously saved, click on the **File** tab and select **Open** or find the file using Windows Explorer and double-click on it.

To close a document click on the **File** tab and select **Exit**.

Save and Save As

To save a document:

- Select **Save** if you have saved the document previously and want to save it with the same filename on the same backing storage.

- Select **Save As** if you want to save the document with a different filename or on different backing storage. For example, you might work on a document and save it on the hard disk on your computer at home, then save it on a memory stick so that you can take it to college and edit it there.

TOP TIP
Always save a document before printing it.

Print

Click on the **File** tab and select **Print**. You can choose which pages to print, the page orientation and page size. There is a **Preview** of one of the pages that will be printed.

Word wrap

Word wrap is what happens when you are typing in text and the last word on the line is automatically moved to the next line.

> ✓ **TOP TIP**
> Press the **Enter** key to start a new paragraph, not to start a new line.

Editing

A word processor provides many useful editing features.

The keyboard

Useful keys for editing text are:

- **Backspace** – deletes text to the left.
- **Delete** – deletes text to the right.
- **Enter** – starts a new paragraph.

Moving text to a different part of the same document or to another document or application

The easiest way to move text is to **drag and drop** it:

1. Select the text using the mouse.
2. Hold down the mouse button and drag the text to its new position.
3. Drop the text by releasing the mouse button.

Another way to move text is to **cut and paste** it:

1. Select the text.
2. Right click and select **Cut**.
3. Move the insertion point to the new position and right click and select **Paste**.

Similarly, you can move content from another application into a document, e.g. you can copy graphs produced in a spreadsheet and paste them into a word processing document.

> - **Cut** removes the original text from the document.
> - **Copy** leaves the original text in the document.

Spelling and grammar checks, and proofreading

Spelling and grammar checkers can check the accuracy of your written English as you type:

- A **spelling checker** identifies each misspelt word and provides a list of possible spellings to choose from.
- A **grammar checker** identifies possible grammatical errors and suggests how these can be corrected.

> ✓ **TOP TIP**
> Spelling and grammar checkers detect most but not all errors and you should proofread your work carefully.

Proofreading is a careful reading of text:

- Look for errors in spelling and grammar that have not been found by spelling and grammar checkers, e.g. *your* instead of *you*.

- Look for missing words and letters, e.g. *a* and *the* are often omitted.

- Check the correct use of capital letters and punctuation marks, especially apostrophes.

- Check homophones (words that sound the same) are used correctly, e.g. *bean* and *been*.

- Make sure that in every sentence the verb and subject agree, e.g. 'she was going to the shops' not 'she were going to the shops'.

Some useful proofreading techniques are:

- Don't rush. You could miss obvious mistakes.

- Check the first sentence and the first paragraph very carefully.

- Check the spelling of unfamiliar words in a dictionary.

- Double-check information that must be accurate, e.g. web addresses.

- Read the text to yourself to help you spot missing words and meaningless sentences.

- Get someone else to check your writing.

Undo and Redo

Undo reverses the last change you made when editing a document. You click on the **Undo** button in the Quick Access Toolbar. **Redo** allows you to undo an undo!

Find and Replace

Find is used to search for a word or phrase in a document. **Replace** is used to replace a word or phrase with a different word or phrase.

Replace All automatically replaces every occurrence of a word or phrase. Using this can be risky, e.g. if you replace all occurrences of 'ion' with 'molecule', words like 'action' become 'actmolecule'!

Formatting

The appearance of a document can be improved using the formatting features.

Character formatting

You can alter the format of characters using the **Home** tab or **Font** dialog box. You can change the:

- Type of **Font**, e.g. Arial or Times New Roman

- Font **Size**, e.g. 12 point or 18 point

- Font **style**, e.g. bold or italic

- Font **Colour**

- Font **Effects**, e.g. strikethrough or superscript. Use **WordArt** for a wider range of effects.

Paragraph formatting

You can alter the format of paragraphs in the **Home** tab or **Paragraph** dialog box. You can change the:

- **Line spacing**, e.g. single or double. You can also alter the spacing between paragraphs, and before and after headings.

- **Alignment**. Paragraphs can be left aligned, centered, right aligned or justified.

- **Indents**. An indent is the distance between the margin and the nearest vertical edge of a paragraph. You can have special indents, e.g. a 'first line' indent has only the first line indented.

- **Tabs**. You can easily indent paragraphs or create columns of text using the Tab key. Put the cursor to the left of the text you want to indent and press the Tab key. You can use Tab several times on one line.

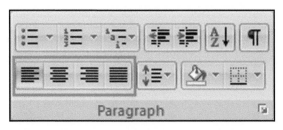

Figure 4.2 *The icons used to left align, center, right align and justify text*

Bullets, numbering and sub-numbering

To add **bullets**, **numbering** or **sub-numbering**, highlight the text and click the appropriate button in the **Home** tab. To alter the style of bullet, numbering or sub-numbering, click on the down arrow to the right of the button.

Page layout

On the **Page Layout** tab, click on the appropriate button and you can change:

- the width of the **Margins**

- the page **Orientation**, e.g. **Portrait** or **Landscape**

- the paper **Size**, e.g. A4 or perhaps because you want to print on envelopes.

On the **Insert** tab, click on the appropriate button and you can:

- Insert a **Header** that appears across the top of every page, or a **Footer** that appears across the bottom of every page.

- Insert **Page Numbers**, e.g. in the Header or Footer.

- Start a new page by inserting a **Page Break**.

Tables

A **table** is made up of **rows** and **columns** and their intersection is called a **cell**. To insert a table, click on the **Insert** tab, then the **Table** button and drag the mouse to set the number of rows and columns.

To insert a row in an existing table:

- Highlight a row.

- Right-click and select **Insert,** then choose **Insert Rows Above** or **Insert Rows Below.**

> You can change column widths and row heights by dragging the frame.

Borders and shading

If you want to show the **gridlines** when you print the document, you need to add **borders**: click on the table, then the **Design** tab. You can choose a built-in **Table Style**. Alternatively, to customise the borders, click on the **Border** button and the **Border and Shading** dialog box appears.

You can shade rows, columns and cells in a variety of colours. To do this:

- Highlight the rows, columns or cells you want to shade.
- Click on the **Shading** tab in the **Borders and Shading** dialog box.
- Choose the **Fill** colour.
- Use the **Patterns** drop-down menu to select the intensity of the fill; e.g. solid or 10%.

Horizontal and vertical alignment

You can change the direction of text in a table cell. Highlight the cell, and in the **Layout** tab repeatedly click on the **Text Direction** button to cycle through the options.

Merge and split cells

The layout of a table can be customised by merging and splitting cells. You can:

- Merge several cells to make one cell. Select the cells, right click and select **Merge Cells**.
- Split a cell vertically. Select the cell, right click and select **Split Cells**. More complex vertical and horizontal cell splitting can be drawn: in the **Insert** tab, click on the **Table** button and select the **Draw Table** option.

Text wrapping around a table

You can change how text outside a table aligns with and wraps around it. Highlight the table, and in the **Layout** tab in the **Table** group, click on **Properties** and select the appropriate alignment.

Columns

Columns are sometimes needed, e.g. for newspapers and indexes. You can specify the number of columns in the **Columns** drop-down list on the **Page Layout** tab.

Columns can be continuous, so the text automatically flows into the top of the next column. Or you can insert a **column break** to control where the column finishes. You can do this using the **Breaks** drop-down list on the **Page Layout** tab.

Templates

You choose a **template** when you set up a new document. Your new document will have the formatting and page layout of the template. Word has a wide range of templates, e.g. for business cards.

To create a template in Word, produce a document with the formatting and page setup you want, and then save the document as a template not as a word processing document: on the **File** tab, select **Save as** and Save as type: Word Template (*.dotx).

Mail merge

Mail merge helps you produce personalised letters and mailing labels without typing each one individually. This is useful for companies that send letters to customers where the body of the letter is the same for all customers but some information is different, e.g. the name and address.

TOP TIP
You can use the step-by-step mail merge wizard in Word to send personalised letters.

Mail merge uses two files:

- a main document (a **standard letter** or **label**)

- a **data source** containing the personal information.

During mail merge, personal information from the data source is inserted into the main document to produce personalised documents.

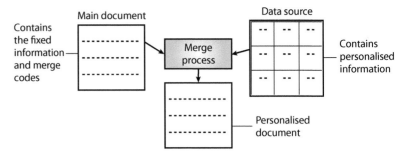

Main document
Contains the fixed information and merge codes

Merge process

Data source
Contains personalised information

Personalised document

Figure 4.3 *How mail merge works*

Graphics

A variety of **graphics** can be included in a document.

- To insert clipart, place the insertion point where you want the clip art, and on the **Insert** tab, select **Clip Art** and find a suitable image.

- To insert a photograph from a digital camera or a scanned image, save it as a file, go to where you want it placing, and on the **Insert** tab, select **Picture** and find the file.

- To insert the whole or a part of the screen, press the **Print Screen** key and the screen display will be copied to the clipboard. You can paste this into a document.

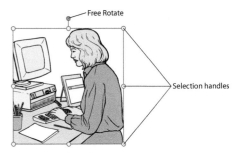

Free Rotate

Selection handles

Figure 4.4 *Selection handles surrounding a graphic*

Click on the graphic and eight selection handles appear. These can be dragged to **rotate** it; and **resize** it by stretching vertically and horizontally, or **enlarging** by dragging a corner handle.

When you **crop** a graphic you trim the edges to remove unwanted parts. Select the picture and on the **Format** tab under **Picture Tools**, in the **Size** group, click on **Crop**.

To **move** a graphic, highlight the graphic and drag it to the desired position, or cut and paste it.

You can put a **border** on a graphic: right click and select **Borders and Shading**.

For some documents, e.g. magazines, you may want text to **wrap** around a graphic as this improves the presentation. Select the graphic and use the **Text Wrapping** options on the **Picture Tools | Format** tab.

Drawing tools

- Word processors include many drawing tools and a variety of shapes, e.g. lines, arrows, callouts; charts and SmartArt. To access these, click on the **Insert** tab.

- A complex illustration can be put together from several smaller clip art or shape objects. To keep the shapes together: hold down Shift and click on each; right click and select **Grouping**, then select **Group**. The objects will now behave as if they were one object and can be copied and moved easily.

- If you insert several objects, they may overlap. You can alter the **order** in which they cover each other: select an object and right click, select **Order** and **Bring to Front**. This places the selected object in front of all other overlapping objects.

- The individual objects that are grouped can be difficult to edit unless you **Ungroup** them. Select the grouped shape, right click, and select **Grouping** then **Ungroup**. You can quickly return to the grouped shape by selecting **Regroup**.

Desktop publishing (DTP)

DTP software, e.g. Microsoft Publisher, is used to produce leaflets, newsletters, newspapers, posters, business cards and many other forms of printed communication.

> DTP and word processing software have many common features – e.g. you can open, save and print documents, enter and edit text, change the font type and size, and insert new pages. The main difference is that when you are setting up a new DTP document you have to decide on the **page layout**. You can do this by selecting a template or inserting objects, e.g. text boxes.

Templates help you create different page layouts. To customise a template, choose from a range of colour schemes on the **Picture Tools Format** tab and edit the text.

Objects are inserted in **frames** and you can insert a:

- **Text box.** Click on the **Draw Text Box** button on the **Home** tab. Dragging the mouse pointer across the page creates a text frame. When you type, the text appears in the text box.

- **Picture.** Click on the **Picture** button on the **Home** tab and choose a picture file.

- **Page layout** is controlled by resizing, rotating and moving frames using the selection handles. You can crop pictures: select the picture and in the **Picture Tools Format** tab select **Crop**. You can also **wrap text** around a graphic and put a **border** on a frame.

- An important feature of DTP is the ability to make **text flow** between linked text boxes that are separate and in different positions on the page or on different pages. Text flow works when you resize frames and when you delete or insert text.

- When a text box is full, the **Text Overflow indicator** appears on the lower right-hand side of the text frame. Click on this and on the page: a new text box is created and text will flow between these frames.

Worked Example

a) A café does not allow customers to smoke. Design a No Smoking sign.

b) The café sells tea, coffee and a variety of snacks. Design a menu.

Answers

a) Microsoft Publisher has a template for a No Smoking sign. Use this and adapt the text for the café.

b) Microsoft Word and Publisher both have templates for a menu. Chose a template and adapt this for the café. Your menu should have an eye-catching title and include the name and contact details for the café. Illustrate it with pictures of some of the drinks and snacks.

1. The type of software used to write a letter is:

    A   presentation

    B   desktop publishing

    C   word processing

    D   operating system   *(1 mark)*

2. Which one of these errors is unlikely to be detected by spelling and grammar checkers?

    A   Their garden has a large beach tree

    B   We do not know weather it will be a fine day

    C   The house is bilt on sand

    D   The hen laid a large eegg   *(1 mark)*

3. Identify one way **Save** is different from **Save as**.

    A   You save the file as a word processing document

    B   You have to use the same filename

    C   The file is saved

    D   You can save the file with a different filename   *(1 mark)*

4. Type the following:

    a) 14th January 2015   *(1 mark)*

    b) H$_2$O   *(1 mark)*

5. Derek Johnson holds a weekly meeting of his sales team at CarsUK. The next meeting will be held on Monday 22nd July at 10.00 am in his office (Room 16). Ann Winters works for Human Resources and Derek wants her to attend the meeting to discuss the new bonus scheme.

    a) Create a memo from Derek to Ann (hint: use a template).   *(1 mark)*

    b) The meeting will include discussion of: current sales and compare these with the previous year; the impact of fuel prices on the sales of new cars; and the introduction of electric cars. Write an agenda for the meeting.   *(1 mark)*

6. You are going to run a car wash to raise money for charity.

    a) Write a letter to the manager of a local supermarket asking for permission to use the car park.   *(4 marks)*

    b) Design a poster advertising the event. *(5 marks)*

7. This is a list of students with their name and their grades in English and Mathematics.

    Paul Johnson, A, B

    Zahid Patel, C, A

    Claire Johnson, B, B

    Ian Crawford, D, C

    Ann Smith, A, C

    Put the data in a table with appropriate headings and improve its appearance.   *(4 marks)*

8. Manor School is having its annual sports day and wishes to invite parents. The principal wants each pupil's parent to receive a personal invitation. The school knows parents' name and addresses. The letters will be given to form teachers to give to pupils to take home.

    a) Describe how this could be done using mail merge.   *(5 marks)*

    b) What data will need to be included in the data source? Produce this for five parents. *(3 marks)*

    c) Design a standard letter that will include the information from the data source. Include a picture of the school.   *(4 marks)*

    d) Run the mail merge and produce five personalised invitations.   *(2 marks)*

TOP TIP ✓

Always use good spelling, punctuation and grammar. You cannot be awarded top marks if the examiner does not understand what you are saying.

Chapter 5: Spreadsheets and modelling

> **You need to know:**
>
> You need to know how to use spreadsheet software, e.g. Microsoft Excel. This chapter reminds you which features of a spreadsheet you should be able to use; however, run the software and make sure you can use it.
>
> - A **spreadsheet** has several worksheets divided into **rows** and **columns.**
> - **Cells** hold different types of information, e.g. labels or formulae.
> - A single cell is referred to using its **cell reference**.
> - A **range** of cells is identified by the cell references of the top left-hand and bottom right-hand cells.
> - Some features of spreadsheets are similar to word processing.
> - In Microsoft Excel, a **formula** starts with an '=', uses cell references, and can include **functions**.
> - A formula can be **copied** or **replicated** into other cells. **Relative cell references** in a formula will change depending on the cell they are copied into; **absolute cell references** do not change.
> - You can **sort** data.
> - A wide range of **graphs and charts** can be produced.
> - **Lookup** tables enable you to store information on one worksheet and refer to it in another.
> - A **macro** is a series of commands that you group together.
> - A **model** is a representation of the real world that can be constructed using a spreadsheet.

Basic concepts

- Spreadsheet software initially displays the **active worksheet.** Other worksheets can be hidden behind it. A worksheet is displayed by clicking on its name tab. You can **rename** a worksheet: right-click on the worksheet tab, select **Rename**, and type in the new name. You can move around a worksheet using the mouse and the cursor control keys.

- Each worksheet has horizontal **rows** which are numbered and vertical **columns** named using letters.

- The intersection of a row and a column is called a **cell.** The cell being edited is the **active cell.** The data enters the cell only when the **Enter** key or an arrow key is pressed.

- To **edit** data, select the cell and edit the content box. To **delete** data, select the cell and press the **Delete** key.

A cell holds different types of data, e.g.:

- A **label** is a title or heading and cannot be used in a calculation. It must start with a character other than '='.

- A **value** is a number that can be used in a calculation.

- A **formula** performs calculations and must start with an '='.

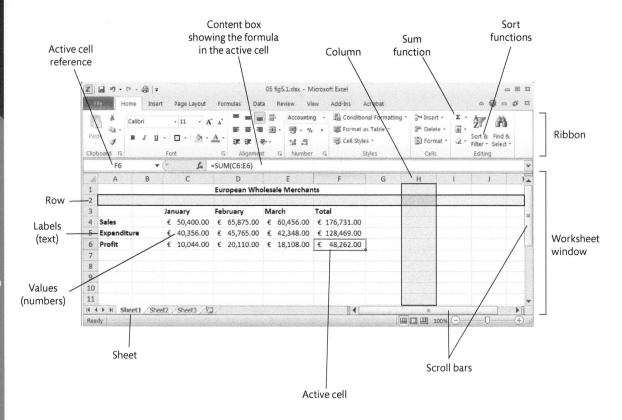

Figure 5.1 *A typical spreadsheet*

Cell references

A cell is identified by its **cell reference**, e.g. F6 means the cell in column F and row 6.

A **cell range reference** refers to a rectangular block of cells:

- E3:E5 is the block including E3, E4 and E5.

- C4:E7 refers to the all the cells in columns C to E that are in rows 4 to 7.

Cell references in one worksheet can **refer to another worksheet**, e.g. **Sheet2!A3** refers to cell A3 in Sheet2. If you wanted to refer to the cell range A3:A11 in Sheet4, you would use **Sheet4!A3:A11.**

Some features similar to word processing software

Some features of spreadsheets are used in similar ways to word processing although there are some differences:

- The **font**, **size** and **style** of text can be changed.

- Pictures and clip art can be imported.

- Alignment can be changed: select the cells and click one of the **Alignment** buttons on the **Home** tab.

- To **cut, copy and paste**, select the cells or chart to be copied. These can be pasted elsewhere in the active worksheet, or into another worksheet, spreadsheet or application.

- To add a **border,** select the cells and on the **Home** tab in the **Font** group select from the **Borders** drop-down menu. For **shading**, select the cells and select from the **Fill Color** drop-down menu.

- To **merge** or **unmerge** cells, select the cells, and on the **Home** tab in the **Alignment** group, select your choice from the **Merge & Center** drop-down menu.

- When you enter too much text in a cell, if it is left aligned it will overflow to the right on the same row. To make the text wrap around in the cell, select the cell and on the **Home** tab in the **Alignment** group select **Wrap** text.

- You can **save**, **open** and **print** in the same way, but you can also print the active worksheet, or the entire workbook, i.e. all the worksheets.

Insert and delete rows and columns

Rows and columns can be inserted and deleted, e.g.:

To **insert a row**:

- Select the row below the row where you want the new row.

- Right-click and select **Insert.**

To **delete a column**:

- Select the column to be deleted.

- Right-click and select **Delete.**

Change column width and row height

To increase the width of column B, click between the column letters B and C. The cursor changes to a vertical bar with horizontal arrows. Drag to the right.

TOP TIP ✓
If ######### is displayed in a cell it may be a value that is too big to be displayed. Increase the column width to see the cell contents.

Formulae

Formulae are used to do calculations based on values in other cells.

Formulae can include **operators**, **cell references** and **functions**:

- Operators include +, −, * (multiply) and / (divide), e.g. =A5−A6

- There can be more than one operator in a formula, e.g. =D3+B7*5.

- The same order of precedence is used as for normal arithmetic. Whatever is within brackets is calculated first, then multiplication and/or division, and then addition and/or subtraction, e.g. 14−3*2 has the value 8.

Formulae use cell references so that if a value in a cell is changed, all the values in the dependent cells are **automatically recalculated.**

TOP TIP ✓
Start formulae with an '=' sign.

Functions

Functions are used in formulae:

- **SUM** is used to add up the values in a group of cells, e.g. = SUM(B3:B9) calculates the sum of rows 3 to 9 in column B. An advantage of using SUM is that if a row is inserted the formula will automatically readjust.

TOP TIP ✓
To add the numbers in cells B3, B4, B5 and B6, *use* =Sum(B3:B6)

Do not use =B3+B4+B5+B6

Do not use =Sum(B3+B4+B5+B6)

- **AVERAGE** is used to find the mean of a set of values,
  e.g. = AVERAGE(B5:D5) finds the average of the values in cells B5, C5 and D5.

- **IF** tests a condition to see if it is true, e.g. =IF(H7> 3,"inflation is high", "inflation is low") places the message "inflation is high" in the cell if H7 has a value greater than 3. If the value is 3 or less, the message "inflation is low" is displayed.

TOP TIP

The AVERAGE function calculates the mean (not the median, or mode).

Example: the mean of 3, 5, 7 and 9 is 6. This is (3+5+7+9)/4

Copying and replication, and relative and absolute cell references

You can cut or copy and paste a formula. You can also **replicate** a formula, e.g. the formula in the active cell is copied to other cells by dragging the fill handle up/down or left/right.

> When copied or replicated, **relative cell references**, e.g. B6, change in relation to the formula's location; whereas if **absolute cell references**, e.g. $B$6 are used, these do not change.
>
> *Example*: suppose the formula =B6*C6 is in cell D6. If this is replicated down column D, D7 would contain the formula, =B7*C7, D8 would contain =B8*C8 and so on.
>
> Suppose the formula =$B$6*C6 is in cell D6. If this is replicated down column D, D7 would contain the formula, =$B$6*C7, D8 would contain =$B$6*C8 and so on.

Formatting values

Some formats for values are:

- **Number**, e.g. –24.5
- **Currency**, e.g. $123.54
- **Percentage**, e.g. 95%
- **Date**, e.g. 24 May 2012 or 24/5/12.
- **Time**, e.g. 10:35:00 pm or 22:35:00.

You can change the formatting of a cell, e.g. to change the format to Currency, select the cells and on the **Home** tab, in the **Number** group, click on the **Currency** button.

Sort

You can sort data into ascending or descending order. **Ascending order** means the lowest value at the top and the highest at the bottom. **Descending order** has the highest value at the top.

Sorting on a single column

Data can be sorted according to the contents of the leftmost column highlighted. To do this, select all the data you wish to sort and on the **Home** tab, click the **Sort & Filter** button and choose **Sort A to Z**.

Sorting on multiple columns

You may wish to sort data by more than one column. For example, people live in different areas and you may want a list of these areas in alphabetic order, with the names of those people who live in them in alphabetic order. Select the data, in the **Home** tab click the **Sort & Filter** button and choose **Custom Sort**. Click on **Copy Level** and **Sort by** the area **Then by** the name.

Graphs and charts

Choosing a graph or chart

The type you should use is affected by the data you want to display. Use:

- a **pie chart to** show data as slices of a whole 'pie';
- a **bar chart** if the horizontal axis has discrete values or categories (e.g. North, South, East, and West) and the vertical axis is a number;
- a **line graph** if both axes are numbers;
- a **scattergram** if you are comparing two sets of discrete values or categories to see if they correlate.

TOP TIP ✓

In Excel, a bar chart has horizontal bars and a column chart has vertical bars. In the UK, in mathematics, a bar chart has vertical bars.

Creating a graph or chart

To create a graph or chart:

- Select the data values. You can plot any row or column of data against any other row or column of data.
- On the **Insert** tab, select an appropriate type of chart.

Chart elements

Chart can have several elements:

- **Axes** – vertical and horizontal lines against which data is plotted.
- **Titles** – for the horizontal and vertical axes, and the chart itself.
- **Data range** – range of cells selected to create the chart.
- **Data labels** – e.g. the name of a bar in a bar chart.
- **Data table** – range of values used to draw the chart. This can be shown at the bottom of the chart.
- **Series** – data in a row or column that makes up the range of values that is used to create the chart.
- **Legend** – cross-reference showing how each series is represented in the chart.
- **Gridlines** – lines parallel to each axis that help you read values from the chart more easily.

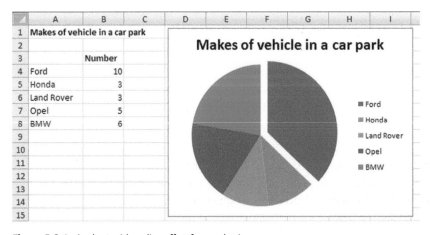

Figure 5.2 *A pie chart with a slice offset for emphasis*

Enhancing a chart

Charts can be customised or enhanced for variety and emphasis, e.g. a slice of a pie chart can be offset from the main body of the pie: click on the slice to be offset, and drag the slice out of the pie. Several features of the slice can be changed, including its colour. Select the slice you wish to change, right-click it and select **Format Data Point.** Select **Fill** then **Solid fill** and select a colour.

You can also customise a chart using the options on the **Chart Tools** tab in the **Design**, **Layout** and **Format** tabs.

Lookup tables

If you know something about a person or object, you can look up other information, e.g. if you know the name of a country, you can look up its population.

The general form of the lookup function is:

> = LOOKUP(*what you are looking for, where you want to look, where the information you want is*)

For example:

> = LOOKUP("Nigeria", B4:B13, C4:C13)

This means look for the word 'Nigeria' in cells B4 to B13. When you find it, display the contents of the corresponding cell from the range C4 to C13. This LOOKUP should return the value 166,629,000. LOOKUP will not work unless the lookup column is sorted into ascending order.

	A	B	C	D
1				
2				
3		Country	Population	
4		Bangladesh	152,518,015	
5		Brazil	193,946,886	
6		China	1,347,350,000	
7		India	1,210,193,422	
8		Indonesia	237,641,326	
9		Japan	127,520,000	
10		Nigeria	166,629,000	
11		Pakistan	181,037,000	
12		Russia	143,228,300	
13		United States	314,642,000	
14				

Figure 5.3 *A lookup table*

Lookup tables are particularly useful when used with multiple worksheets. You can store information on one worksheet and refer to it in another; and you can use the results calculated in one worksheet as part of a calculation in another worksheet.

TOP TIP ✓
Hide a lookup table in another worksheet.

Macros

Macros help you automate tasks that you do repeatedly.

To create a macro:

- Make sure the **Developer** tab is visible: if not, on the **Office Button**, select **Excel Options** then the **Popular** category. Click on **Show Developer tab in the Ribbon**.

- On the **Developer** tab click on **Record Macro**.

- Give the macro a **name**, e.g. 'Title', and click on **OK**. Everything you do before you turn off the macro recorder is recorded.

- In Sheet1, Highlight cells A1 to G1 and on the **Home** tab, click on **Merge and Center** and change the **Fill Color, Font Color** and **Font Size.**

- On the **Developer** tab click on **Stop Recording.**

TOP TIP ✓
You can assign macros to keyboard shortcuts and this can be a very convenient way of running a macro: on the **Developer** tab select **Macros** and select **Macro name**: Title. Click the **Options** button and enter the **Shortcut key** Ctrl + h. Pressing Ctrl + h on the keyboard will now run the macro.

To run the macro you have created:

- In Sheet2, type in a title in cell A1.

- On the **Developer** tab, select **Macro** and select the macro **named 'Title'**. Click **Run**.

Modelling

Models are representations of the real world that can help you learn about unfamiliar situations, develop skills without danger or expense, and forecast what will happen. A model can be such a good representation of reality that we can use it for training. For example, pilots are trained using simulators before flying real aircraft.

Spreadsheet models

When a model is constructed using a spreadsheet, there is usually an intention to use it to improve our understanding of a real system, for problem solving or for prediction.

A spreadsheet-based model is likely to:

- allow several **input variables** to be set;

- use formulae to define the **rules** on which the model is based;

- produce **output** based on the input variables and the rules.

Example: a Price Forecast model could be used to work out what a car would cost in 10 years' time.

- The input variables are the price of the car (£9,500), the base year (2013), and the rate of inflation (2.6%). The spreadsheet is set up so that these inputs can be changed.

- The rules are in cells D7 to D16:

  - D7=A4

  - D8=D7*$E$4+D7

  - D8 is replicated in cells D9 to D16, so that, e.g. D14=D13*$E$4+D13

    - The absolute cell reference $E$4 is used so that the formulae refer to the same rate of inflation in cell E4.

- The output is the price year by year. The price of the car in 10 years is shown as £11,968.78.

This model has some limitations. The rate of inflation is assumed to be constant for 10 years and this is very unlikely. This assumption is needed so that a simple, understandable model can be constructed.

	A	B	C	D	E
1	**Price Forecast model**				
2					
3	**Initial Price**		**Base year**		**Inflation**
4	£ 9,500.00		2013		2.6%
5					
6			Year	Price	
7			2013	£ 9,500.00	
8			2014	£ 9,747.00	
9			2015	£10,000.42	
10			2016	£10,260.43	
11			2017	£10,527.20	
12			2018	£10,800.91	
13			2019	£11,081.74	
14			2020	£11,369.86	
15			2021	£11,665.48	
16			2022	£11,968.78	
17					

Figure 5.4 *Price Forecast model*

A mechanic receives a wage of $350 per week. This is what the mechanic expects to spend.

	Monday	Tuesday	Wednesday	Thursday	Friday	Saturday	Sunday
Travelling	8	8	8	8	8	10	0
Lunch	6	7	7	7	9	10	8
Snacks	2	2	1	2	2	3	2
Entertainment	3	5	5	6	5	30	10

Using a spreadsheet, enter the above data, and:

a)   Improve its appearance.

b)   Calculate the total money spent each day of the week.

c)   Calculate the total money spent on each category for the week.

d)   Calculate total spending for the week.

e)   The mechanic pays 20% tax on earnings above $100. Calculate the amount paid in tax.

f)   Calculate the amount left from the mechanic's wage after tax and spending are deducted.

g)   The mechanic saves 30% of the remainder. Use the spreadsheet to work out how much the mechanic saves each week.

Answers

Budget for a wage of $350								
	Monday	Tuesday	Wednesday	Thursday	Friday	Saturday	Sunday	Totals
Travelling	$8.00	$8.00	$8.00	$8.00	$8.00	$10.00	$–	$50.00
Lunch	$6.00	$7.00	$7.00	$7.00	$9.00	$10.00	$8.00	$54.00
Snacks	$2.00	$2.00	$1.00	$2.00	$2.00	$3.00	$2.00	$14.00
Entertainment	$3.00	$5.00	$5.00	$6.00	$5.00	$30.00	$10.00	$64.00
Total	$19.00	$22.00	$21.00	$23.00	$24.00	$53.00	$20.00	$182.00

Tax	$50.00
Amount left after tax and spending	$118.00
Weekly savings	$35.40

1. Which of the following is **not** an example of modelling?

   A Using a spreadsheet to predict profits

   B Learning to drive a car using a simulator

   C Working out the impact of different rates of inflation on family income

   D Sorting a list of names into alphabetic order using a spreadsheet   *(1 mark)*

2. When would a spreadsheet be used?

   A To write a letter

   B To edit a photograph

   C To work out a budget for a holiday

   D To format a disk   *(1 mark)*

3. Which of the following are false?

   A The intersection of a row and a column is a cell

   B The formula =$H$7*$E$7 will not change when it is copied

   C If the value in cell C7 changes, the value of the formula =D8+G15 changes automatically

   D A cell can be formatted for currency   *(1 mark)*

TOP TIP

In question 3, read each option carefully and decide whether it is true or false.

4. The Harriers Running Club records the performance of some of its members. Times are in minutes for a 1 km and 10 km race.

Jones	2.3	50.8
Smith	4.5	40.7
Patel	3.6	32.5
Singh	6.9	45.6
Shoard	2.7	31
McGuire	3.9	30.1

   Using a spreadsheet, enter the data, and:

   a) Improve its appearance.   *(3 marks)*

   b) Sort the data so that the runner who is fastest in the 1 km race appears at the top of the list.   *(1 mark)*

   c) Sort the data so that the runner who is fastest in the 10 km race appears at the top of the list.   *(1 mark)*

   d) Draw a chart showing the performance of the runners in both races.   *(4 marks)*

   e) The club has to choose one runner to run in a 5 km race. Which runner should they choose? Explain your answer.   *(2 marks)*

5. The income a shop in France makes on some of the items it sells is shown in Euros.

	Groceries	**Drinks**	**Bread**	**Newspapers**
Monday	345	76	321	79
Tuesday	658	78	477	73
Wednesday	474	58	588	56
Thursday	664	65	344	34
Friday	998	87	435	89
Saturday	546	65	325	45
Sunday	45	435	565	348

   Using a spreadsheet, enter the above data, and:

   a) Improve the appearance of the spreadsheet.   *(4 marks)*

   b) Calculate the total income each day.   *(1 mark)*

   c) Calculate the total income on each category for the week.   *(1 mark)*

   d) Calculate total income for the week.   *(2 marks)*

   e) The shop pays 20% VAT on total income. What is the income after VAT?   *(2 marks)*

   f) The shopkeeper has estimated that after 10 years, an income of around €11,000 after VAT will be needed. Use your spreadsheet to find the annual rate of increase necessary to achieve this.   *(2 marks)*

Chapter 6: Databases

> **You need to know:**
>
> You need to know how to use **database** software, e.g. Microsoft Access. This chapter reminds you which features of this software you should be able to use; however, run the software and make sure you can use it.
>
> - A **database** is an organised collection of structured data.
> - A **record** is a group of related fields, e.g. information about a person. A **field** is a data item within a record, e.g. surname.
> - A **table** is an organised collection of records about similar subjects. Each row is a **record** and each column is a **field**.
> - A **relational** database has several linked tables.
> - Tables can be set up using a **template** or in **Datasheet View** or **Design View**.
> - A **key field (primary key)** uniquely identifies a record.
> - A field's **data type** determines what type of data it can store, e.g. date/time.
> - **Field properties** include **validation** checks, e.g. a range check.
> - Data can be **input** by: entering it in a table; using an input form; or importing it from another application.
> - A **query** searches a database. There are several types of query, e.g. a Select query.
> - A **report** is an attractive display of the information from the database.

Creating a database

Database software enables you to organise, store, search and report. Databases are widely used, e.g. to track students' progress in schools and to produce personalised mail sent to business customers.

To **create** a database in Access, run the software and select **New** from the **File** tab. Select a blank database or a template and double click.

The database objects available are listed in the **All Access Objects** panel. The objects used in this chapter are:

Object	Description
Table	A collection of related data about similar subjects.
	A **flat file** database has one table, whereas a **relational database** has more than one table.
Query	Used to **search** a database.
Report	A customised printout of information from a table or query.

Designing a database

The steps involved in designing a database are:

- State the **purposes** of the database, e.g. I need to be able to contact students in an emergency.
- Decide **what data is needed**, e.g. for each student I need their name and telephone number.
- **Design** the tables and records. You may need separate tables for the students' personal details and their academic record.

Tables

- A table is divided into **rows** and **columns**. Each row is a **record** and each column is a **field**.

- A **record** is a group of related fields, e.g. the information about one student.

- A **field** is a data item within a record, e.g. a student's first name. Every field must have a fieldname and properties, e.g. the fieldname is FIRSTNAME; the data type is alphabetic; and the field length is 15 characters.

- A **key field** (**primary key**) uniquely identifies a record, e.g. STUDENTID.

TOP TIP ✓
A flat file database has only one table, whereas a relational database has several linked tables.

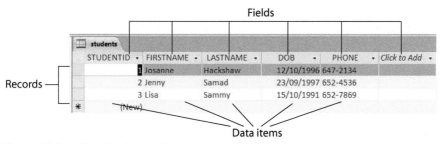

Figure 6.1 *Part of a table about students*

Creating tables

You can create a table in different ways:

- Using a **template** – these already have a data structure. If they are suitable for your needs you can set up a database using one and edit it. On the **File** tab, select **New** and select from the available templates.

- In **Datasheet View** – you enter data into the datasheet grid, which consists of rows and columns labelled *Field1, Field2, Field3* and so on.

- In **Design View** – you name fields and select their data types and their properties.

Creating a table in Design View

Click on the **Create** tab then on **Table Design,** and the **Table Design View** window appears. Create the fields you want, then on the **File** tab, **Save** the table.

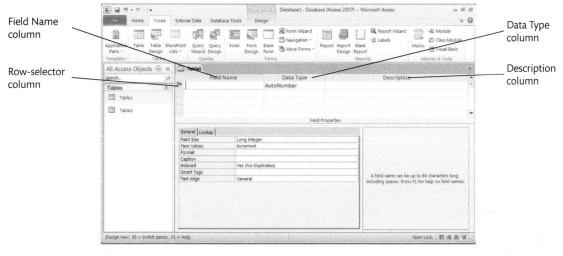

Figure 6.2 *The Table Design View window*

You create fields in the **Table Design View** window using four columns:

- **Row selector** – selects the field.
- **Field Name** – type in a field name.
- **Data Type** – select the data type from a drop-down list. When you have selected a data type, the **Field Properties** pane appears. You can edit the default field properties.
- **Description** – enter information about this field.

Some **data types** are:

- **Real number** – a decimal number, e.g. 54.371, –9.78
- **Integer** – a whole number, e.g. 15, –9
- **Alphanumeric** or **Text** – any alphabetic or numeric character, punctuation marks and other special characters.
- **Date/Time** – the date or time in different formats, e.g. DD/MM/YYYY, MM/DD/YY.
- **Logical** or **Boolean** – one of two values, e.g. 1 or 0; true or false.
- **AutoNumber** – generates unique numbers.

You can **edit a record** in **Design View**, e.g. to insert a field – select a row below where the new field is to be inserted. Right-click and select **Insert Rows**.

Primary keys

To make a field a **primary key**, in **Design View**, select the field, right click and select **Primary Key**.

Using a primary key you can:

- Establish relationships between tables. You can link tables so queries can retrieve data from several tables.
- Speed up data retrieval and queries.

To deselect a primary key, in **Design View** select the primary key field. On the **Table Tools | Design** tab, click on the **Primary Key** button to deselect the primary key.

A **foreign key** is a primary key from another table. It links the current table to the table where it is the primary key. A record has only one primary key, but can have many foreign keys.

Field properties

A field's properties determine how it is stored, what can be done with it and how it is displayed.

Validation checks

Validation check	Description of field property and validation check
Range	The **Validation Rule** property checks that values in a field are within a specified range, e.g. >0 checks that a number is bigger than zero. The **Validation text** is the message displayed if the validation rule is not satisfied, e.g. you have spent all the money in your bank account.
Presence	The **Required** property checks that there is a value present in a field. If not, the record is rejected and an error message displayed, e.g. Date of birth is required.
Type	The data entered must agree with the **Data Type**, e.g. if the data type is Number you cannot enter text.
Length	A length check ensures that the **Field Size** is less than its maximum, e.g. a student's first name might be given a field size of 14.

Entering data

You enter data in a table in Datasheet View. To enter a new record, fill in the fields in the blank record at the bottom of the table.

Entering data using an input form

Select the table you wish to enter data into and on the **Create** tab, click on the **Form** button. An input form is created.

- To input a new record, click the **New (blank) record** button and enter the data.

- To edit, use **search** to find the record you want to edit or use the **Previous record** and **Next record** buttons.

Sort

To sort on a **single** field, open the table in **Datasheet View** and select the field, then click the **Sort Ascending** or **Sort Descending** button on the **Home** tab.

To sort a table on **multiple** fields, e.g. to sort a list of students by their last name and then by their first name:

- On the **Home** tab, in the **Sort & Filter** group, select **Advanced** and then **Advanced Filter/Sort.** The **Filter** tab appears. The top part of the tab displays the table to be sorted and the bottom part has a grid to select the fields to be sorted.

- Click in the first box in the **Field** row and select the field you would like sorted. Click on the corresponding sort field to select the sort order. Do this for as many fields as you wish to sort on.

- To sort the table, in the **Advanced** drop-down list, select **Apply Filter/Sort.**

Queries

- A **query** is used to search a database and extract information stored in one or more tables. Queries can be saved and reused.

- **Select queries** are the most common type but there a several other types, e.g. Update queries. Select queries search tables, retrieve data and display the results.

- To run a query, create or open it, then on the **Query Tools | Design** tab in the **Results** group, click the **Run** button.

Creating a Select query

Open the database and on the **Create** tab click on the **Query Design** button.

The **Show Table** dialog box appears with the **Query Design** tab behind it. In the **Show Table** dialog box you select the tables to be included in the query. On the **Tables** tab, select the required tables and click **Add** and they appear in the upper part of the **Query Design** tab. You can also drag tables from the **Tables** panel.

To remove a table, select the table in the **Query Design** tab, right click and select **Remove Table.**

Creating relationships between tables

A query can be made on a single table but if you want to extract data from more than one table, you have to create a relationship between the tables.

To create a relationship:

- In the **Database Tools** tab, select **Relationships** and the **Relationships** tab and the **Show Table** dialog box appears. **Add** the tables between which you want to create a relationship.

- On the **Relationships** tab, drag the field name in one table and drop it on a field name in the other table. The **Edit Relationships** dialog box appears, showing the names of the two tables and the fields you would like to join. Click on **OK.** A line connecting the two fields is displayed in the **Relationships** tab.

- Save the relationship.

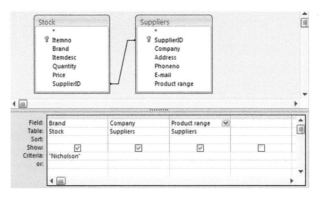

Figure 6.3 *A Select Query design tab, showing a relationship between tables*

Setting up search criteria

You create the search criteria in the bottom part of the **Query Design** tab by setting up each row.

Row label	Explanation
Field	Select the field to be searched.
Table	Select the table that the selected field is taken from.
Sort	If you want the results sorted, select the fields to sort on and select **Ascending** or **Descending**.
Show	The **Show** row contains a check box in each column. Tick the box if you would like the value of the field shown in the results.
Criteria	To specify selection criteria, enter **values** or **expressions** in the **Criteria** rows. An expression can include **relational operators**, e.g. >, and **logical operators**, e.g. NOT. The logical operation **AND** applies to criteria on the same row, and **OR** applies to criteria in the same column.
	AND tests two or more criteria, and if they are **all** individually true, then AND is true.
	OR tests two or more criteria, and if **at least one of them** is individually true, then the OR is true.

Reports

A report displays the contents of a table or the results of a query for displaying on the screen or printing. It includes:

- A **report header** is displayed at the beginning of the report and includes, e.g. the title.

- A **page header** appears after the report header and at the top of every other page. It includes page numbers and column headings, which by default are the field names.

- If the records are sorted into groups, a **group header** is placed before the first record in the group and a **group footer** after the last.

- A **page footer** is the last item on each page and includes, e.g. a page number.

- A **report footer** appears at the bottom of the report. It includes summary values, e.g. the number of records.

Creating a report

A quick way to create a simple report is to select a table or query and on the **Create** tab click on the **Report** button. The report is displayed in a **Report** tab. You can use the tools in the **Report Layout Tools | Design**, **Arrange**, **Format** and **Page Setup** tabs to edit the report.

Alternatively, you could use the **Report Wizard**. On the **Create** tab, click on the **Report Wizard** button and a dialog box appears. If you follow the wizard, you can:

- Select the tables or queries that contain the fields to be displayed in the report.

- Select the fields to be displayed in the report.

- Decide whether to group the output.

- Sort the report on up to four fields in ascending or descending order.

- Decide how to layout the report.

- Choose the font style.

- Type in a title for the report.

- Click on **Finish** to create the report.

Loading data created in another application

Data imported into a database is often created in another application. For example, to create a database table from a **.csv** (comma-separated variables) file created in a spreadsheet:

- On the **File** tab, select **Open,** select the file, and click on **Open.**

- The **Link Text Wizard** dialog box appears. Follow this through. Choose the field delimiter and name each field.

- Click on the **Finish** button and the file is imported into a database table.

Worked Example

A database is used to store information about employees.

a) Create an EMPLOYEES table:

Field name	Data type	Description
EMPID	Text	Unique ID for each employee
LNAME	Text	Last name of an employee
FNAME	Text	First name of an employee
JOB	Text	Employee's job
SALARY	Currency	Annual salary

b) Enter this data in the table:

EMPID	LNAME	FNAME	JOB	SALARY (£)
140	Moor	Mary	Manager	42,000.00
252	Johnson	Amite	Cleaner	12,500.00
346	Chong	Lisa	Engineer	28,000.00
556	Sakkara	Mary	Engineer	28,000.00
553	Vieira	John	Programmer	36,000.00
231	Moor	Kohl	Secretary	20,000.00
125	Louis	Sheba	Systems Analyst	39,000.00
813	Bath	Allan	Secretary	21,500.00
143	Griffin	Sean	Engineer	29,500.00
133	Alexander	Lisa	Cleaner	13,000.00

c) Create a data entry form. Make sure it has a suitable title and is clear and easy to use. A new employee has started work. She is called Jennie Barstow, she is an engineer and her salary will be £25,000. Enter her details using the data entry form and give her a suitable ID.

d) Enter at least four more records using the form.

e) Sort the table into alphabetic order on the employee's last name. Provide evidence that you have done this.

f) A director wants a list of employees earning over £25,000. Create a query on the EMPLOYEES table to find the correct records. Sort these into descending order on SALARY. Produce a suitable report showing the first and last names of the employee, their job and the salary they earn.

TOP TIP
Evidence is a screen shot of the data entry form with Jennie Barstow's details in it. Insert it in a word processor document and explain what it is.

Answers

a) to f) Suitable evidence would be a screen shot of the data entry form and a screen shot of the sorted table. These should be pasted into a word processing document and you should explain what each screen shot is.

g) The report generated is shown in Figure 6.4. A screen shot of this should be pasted into a word processing document and you should explain what it is.

Employees with a salary over £25,000   07 September 2012
                                                   12:46:43

Last Name	First Name	Job	Salary
Moor	Mary	Manager	£42,000.00
Louis	Sheba	Systems Analyst	£39,000.00
Vieira	John	Programmer	£36,000.00
Gargrave	Donna	Programmer	£32,000.00
Griffin	Sean	Engineer	£29,500.00
Sakkara	Mary	Engineer	£28,000.00
Chong	Lisa	Engineer	£28,000.00

Page 1 of 1

Figure 6.4 *The report*

1. A garage stores customer information. The type of software used would be:

    A database

    B word processing

    C graphics

    D web browser   *(1 mark)*

2. Which of these statements is true?

    A A primary key cannot be used more than 5 times

    B Each row must have two primary keys

    C A primary key has the same value throughout a table

    D A primary key has a value that occurs only once in a column   *(1 mark)*

3. Which term is **not** used to describe how information is organised in a database table?

    A field

    B folder

    C row

    D column   *(1 mark)*

4. A supermarket uses a database to store information about every item it sells. Every item has a barcode on it and this is scanned at the checkout. What item of data must be stored in the bar code?

    A a record

    B a template

    C a primary key

    D a query   *(1 mark)*

5. A database is used to record hotel bookings. There are two linked tables: HOTEL and CUSTOMER.

    a) Create the HOTEL table:

Field name	Data type	Description
HOTELID	Text	A unique ID for each hotel
HNAME	Text	The name of the hotel
HCITY	Text	The city the hotel is in
HRATE	Currency	The cost of a room

    (2 marks)

    b) Enter this data in the table:

HOTELID	HNAME	HCITY	HRATE
PL01	Park	London	$260
PN34	Palace	New York	$300
AP27	Arc	Paris	$250
PD02	Plaza	Delhi	$180
BL77	Bank	London	$130
MM89	Park	Manila	$150

    (2 marks)

    c) Create a data entry form. Make sure it has a suitable title and is clear and easy to use.   *(1 mark)*

    d) Enter the details for the Hotel Continental in Cairo. The room rate is $140. Choose a suitable customer number.   *(2 marks)*

    e) Enter at least four more records.   *(1 mark)*

    f) Provide evidence that you have done this.   *(1 mark)*

    g) A customer wants a list of hotels charging less than $200 per night. Create a query on the HOTEL table to find the correct records. Sort these into ascending order on HRATE. Produce a suitable report showing the name of the hotel, where it is and the rate and print this on one A4 page.   *(4 marks)*

Chapter 6: Databases

h) Create the CUSTOMER table:

Field name	Data type	Description
CUSTID	Text	A unique ID for each customer
LNAME	Text	Last name of customer
FNAME	Text	First name of customer
PHONE	Text	Telephone number of customer
HOTELID	Text	The ID of the hotel the customer has booked
PAID	Boolean	Whether customer has paid in full (Yes/No)

(2 marks)

i) Enter this data in the table:

CUSTID	LNAME	FNAME	PHONE	HOTELID	PAID
102	Ali	Fyzool	+44 12746483216	PL01	Yes
532	Barnes	David	+44 14846492546	PN34	Yes
273	Lara	Leanne	+33 565253359	PL01	Yes
874	King	Mary	+41 276779784	PL01	No
905	Singh	Vishnu	+33 524387099	MM89	Yes

(2 marks)

j) Create a data entry form. Make sure it has a suitable title and is clear and easy to use. *(1 mark)*

k) Enter the details for Mrs Jean King, telephone number +44 1484487265. She is staying at the Plaza in Delhi and has paid for her hotel room. Choose a suitable customer number. *(2 marks)*

l) Enter at least four more records. *(1 mark)*

m) Sort the table in ascending order of LNAME. *(1 mark)*

n) Provide evidence that you have done this. *(1 mark)*

o) A tourism officer wants a report showing which customers are staying in London, at which hotels and whether they have paid. Create a query that searches the HOTEL and CUSTOMER tables. The report should include the name of the hotel, where it is, the first and last names of each customer and whether they have paid. The list should be in alphabetic order on their last name. Produce a suitable report and print this on one A4 page. *(4 marks)*

Chapter 7: Graphics, video and audio editing software

> **You need to know:**
>
> You need to know how to use **graphics** software, and **video** and **audio editing** software. This chapter reminds you which features of this software you should be able to use; however, run the software and make sure you can use it.
>
> - **Graphics** software enables you to create and edit pictures.
> - You can copy the whole screen or the active window using **Print Screen**.
> - Graphic images can be **bit mapped** or **vector**.
> - **Video editing** software is used to produce a movie. A **project** is built up by importing whole videos or video clips or other resources and placing them on a **timeline** or **storyboard** and editing them. When the editing is complete, the project is saved as a **movie,** which can be played on media players.
> - **Audio editing software** is used to record speech, sound or live music and edit it. An **audio file** is produced and this can be played on media players or imported into video editing software.

Graphics

With **graphics software**, e.g. Microsoft Paint and Adobe Photoshop, you can:

- **Create**, **save**, **open** and **print** graphics files.
- **Draw** on the screen using a variety of **colours** and **brushes**, e.g. pencil or airbrush.
- Draw **freehand** shapes and generate **regular shapes**, e.g. circles.
- **Fill** shapes with patterns or colours.
- Insert **text** in different fonts and sizes, and use **word art**.
- **Zoom** in and out.
- **Select** parts of the image, freehand or in blocks.
- **Move, cut, copy** and **paste** blocks.
- **Import** images, e.g. from a scanner or digital camera.
- Use **erasers** of different sizes and shapes to delete parts of the image.
- **Crop** the image, that is, remove the outer edges.

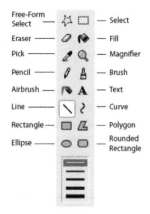

Figure 7.1 *The toolbox in Microsoft Paint*

You can **copy the image on the screen**. This is very useful when you write user guides.

- To copy the **whole screen**, press the **Print Screen** key. This copies an image of the screen into the **Clipboard**. You can paste this into graphics software and edit the image or paste it directly into other applications, e.g. Word.
- To copy the **active window** or a **dialog box**, hold down the **Alt** key and press **Print Screen.** Only the active window is copied to the Clipboard.

Bit-mapped graphics are used for photographs and similar images. High-resolution bit-mapped images are very clear and detailed. However, they have much a bigger file size than low-resolution images. If they are enlarged or zipped and unzipped, the detail of the image can become unclear. Typical file types are **.jpg** and **.bmp**.

Vector graphics are used to produce clip art, and graphs, e.g. in a spreadsheet. When resized, vector graphics use the same storage space and image quality is retained. Vector graphics are produced using mathematical codes, e.g. to represent a square the coordinates of its corners are stored. To enlarge it, the coordinates are changed. Typical file types are .pdf and .wmf.

Video editing software

With **video editing** software, e.g. Adobe Premiere and Microsoft Movie Maker, you can:

- Make a movie by constructing a **project**. To do this you insert whole videos or video clips or other resources on a **timeline** or **storyboard.**

- **Import** whole videos or video clips, pictures, audio clips, music and sound recordings from camcorders, digital cameras and smart phones.

- **Edit** the project. Video clips can be **split**, **combined**, **trimmed**, **moved** and **deleted** from the storyboard.

- Perform **audio editing**, e.g. **fade in** and **volume adjustment**, but more extensive sound editing facilities are available in audio editing software.

- **Insert titles**, **transitions** and **credits**. A transition controls the way that a clip merges into the next clip when a movie is played.

- Insert **effects**, e.g. split screen or black and white movie.

- **Open**, **edit** and **Save** the project.

- When complete, save the project as a **movie**, e.g. as a **.wmv** file.

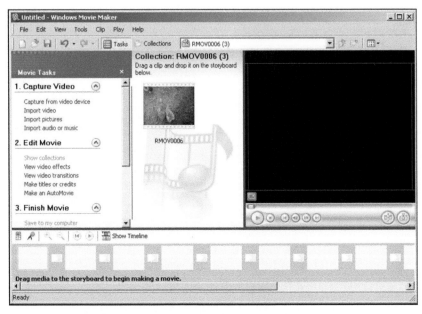

Figure 7.2 *The opening screen of Microsoft Windows Movie Maker*

Audio editing software

With **audio editing software**, e.g. Audacity, you can:

- Make an audio file by constructing a **project**. When complete, the project is saved as an **audio** file, e.g. **.wav** or **.mp3** file.

- **Import** an audio file, e.g. recorded music.

- **Record sound**, e.g. using a **microphone**.

- Adjust the **volume** at which the input is recorded and the output played.

- Record input in **mono** (one channel) or **stereo** (two channels) or more channels.

- Adjust the **quality** of the recorded sound by adjusting the **sampling rate**. Sound is recorded as analogue and is converted to digital by sampling. Sampling is the recording of sound at very small, regular time intervals. The smaller these intervals are, the better the quality of the digital sound but the bigger the sound file.

- Display a **visual illustration** of the recorded sound, for example, a waveform (see Figure 7.3).

- **Play** one or more channels or sound clips.

- **Select** a sound clip and **copy, cut and paste** it from one position to another on the timeline or between channels. You can use this feature to repeat sections.

- **Generate silence**, white noise and other tones.

- **Fade in or out** of a clip, e.g. fade out a crowd laughing.

- **Remove noise**, e.g. remove the hiss from a noisy microphone pre-amplifier input.

Some uses of audio editing software are to:

- Record **voice-overs** for a movie.

- **Improve** recorded sound, e.g. when importing music from legacy media, such as vinyl, there may be background noise or extended silences at the start and end of tracks. These can be edited out.

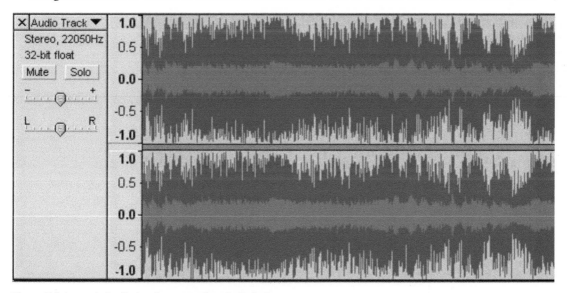

Figure 7.3 *A sound clip displayed as a waveform in Audacity*

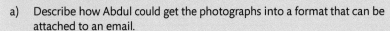

Worked Example

Abdul employed a photographer to take pictures at his wedding. Afterwards, the photographer gave Abdul printed copies. Abdul wants to send copies of the photographs to relatives who live overseas.

a) Describe how Abdul could get the photographs into a format that can be attached to an email.

b) Should Abdul produce high-resolution or low-resolution images? Give reasons for your answer.

TOP TIP

The more explanation and detail you give in an answer, the more likely it is that you will be awarded top marks.

Answers

a) Abdul should use a scanner to input the printed photographs and output them as graphic files, e.g. .jpg.

b) Abdul should scan them as high-resolution images if they are going to be printed or edited overseas as this will ensure the highest quality image. However, high-resolution images generate larger file sizes so they will take longer to send by email, and may be blocked by the ISP because they exceed the file size permitted for email attachments. If the photographs will only be viewed on screen, then low resolution images may be best.

Exam-Style Questions

1. A piece of clip art is saved as a vector graphic. Which of these statements is true?

    A   A large vector graphic needs the same storage space as a small vector graphic.

    B   Vector graphics are usually movies.

    C   When you enlarge a vector graphic the image becomes blurred.

    D   Vector graphics are most suitable for photographs. **(1 mark)**

2. A digital camera saves photos on a memory card. The photos can be saved as high- or low-resolution images. What would be a consequence of saving the photos as low-resolution images?

    A   The photos would be in black and white

    B   You would not be able to use graphics software to edit the photos

    C   The photos would be more secure

    D   More images could be stored on the memory card **(1 mark)**

3. Which feature is not usually found in audio editing software?

    A   Display a sound as a waveform

    B   Airbrush

    C   Adjust the sampling rate

    D   Import a music file **(1 mark)**

4. Which feature is not usually found in video editing software?

    A   Titles and credits

    B   Insert a table

    C   Storyboard

    D   Transitions **(1 mark)**

5. Create a logo for a new sports centre. The logo will be used on the website and on letters and flyers. Make sure the logo is fit for purpose. **(8 marks)**

TOP TIP

Make sure the logo relates to the sports centre.

6. Take a photograph of a friend.

    a) Crop the photograph so that it is more like a passport photograph. Edit the background so that it is a single colour or pattern. **(2 marks)**

    b) Add your friend's name to the image and save it. **(1 mark)**

7. Write a user guide to get a novice started using video editing software. **(6 marks)**

Chapter 8: Presentation software

Presentation software

Examples of presentation software include Microsoft PowerPoint, which is used in this chapter; Impress, which is part of OpenOffice; and Prezi, which is online.

Slides and Notes

- Open Microsoft PowerPoint. You will see a template for an introductory slide. Enter the **title of the presentation**.

- Now add the **slides** that make up your presentation. Right click and select **New Slide**. The default slide **layout** has a title and a large text box. The text you enter in the text box is bulleted and needs to be in a large enough font so it is readable by the audience.

- You may want to write detailed notes to refer to during the presentation. You can do this for each slide in the **Notes pane** at the bottom of the **Normal** view (select this in the **View** tab).

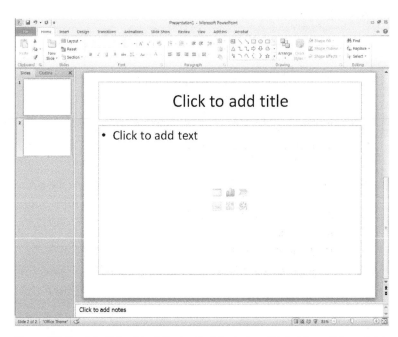

Figure 8.1 *The default for slides following the introductory slide in Microsoft PowerPoint*

Insert text boxes, images and charts

On the **Insert** tab you can:

- Insert text boxes. Select **Text Box**, drag on the slide and type in text. You can **move** and **resize** text boxes, and **restyle the text** as you would in a word processor.

- Insert images e.g. **clip art** and **pictures**. You can **move**, **rotate** and **resize** these.

- Insert and modify charts. Select **Chart** and edit the **Insert Chart** dialog box. To alter the data which is displayed in the chart, you edit the data in Excel. You can also insert charts by cutting and pasting from a spreadsheet.

You can add **animation** to an image: select the image and on the **Animations** tab, select an **Animation Style**, e.g. Wheel. You can also add animation to the title or a line of text, or add several animations to one object.

Layouts, themes, colour schemes and slide transitions

You can select a different layout for a new slide in the **Layout** drop-down menu in the **Slides** group on the **Home** tab; alternatively, you can move and resize the text boxes.

You can select from a range of slide **themes**. In the **Design** tab, hover over a theme to preview it and then click on the one you wish to choose. You can change the **colours** used in the theme in the **Colors** drop-down menu.

A **slide transition** takes place as you move from one slide to the next. The default transition displays the next slide instantly. You can choose a different transition: on the **Animations** tab select the **Transition to This slide**, e.g. Shrink & Turn. You can change the speed of the transition and add a sound (e.g., a drum roll) which plays during the transition. To use the same transition between all the slides in the presentation, click on **Apply To All.**

> **TOP TIP** ✓
> Animation can attract the audience's attention, but too much can confuse and distract.

Links

During a presentation you may want to refer to materials that are not a part of your presentation, e.g. to a website, or audio or video files.

- To insert a **link to a website,** in the **Insert** tab select **Hyperlink,** and complete the dialog box. If your computer is connected to the Internet, during the slide show you can click on this link and the web page will be displayed. To return to your presentation, close the web browser.

- To insert a **link to a file**, e.g. a word processing document, the technique is the same but you select a file.

Master slides

By creating and editing a **master slide**, you can design the layout and other features that are applied to all new slides, e.g. a footer that includes the **date and time, footer text** and **automatic page numbering**.

> **TOP TIP** ✓
> Master slides are not normally visible. To display them, on the **View** tab, select **Slide Master.**

To insert the date and time in a footer on the master slide, on the **Insert** tab, select **Header and Footer**. In the dialog box, select **Footer** and **Date and time**. Click on **Apply to All.**

Whatever is shown on a master slide cannot be changed when editing a slide. By default, there is one slide master but you can create others.

Open, save and print

- To open a presentation, on the **File** tab, select **Open** and select the presentation to be opened in the dialog box. **Save** and **Save As** work in a similar way.

- To print your presentation, on the **File** tab select **Print**. If you click on the **Print** button the default settings will print all your slides one to a page. For handouts, you can print six or more slides on a page, or you can print Notes Pages for the presenter.

Present a slide show

To show the whole presentation, on the **Slide Show** tab select **From Beginning.** Left-click on the mouse to move to the next slide, and to end the slide show, right-click and select **End Show.**

> **TOP TIP** ✓
>
> When you are editing a presentation, you can show it in one window and edit it in another.

Worked Example

Prepare a slide show to provide information about activities at a gym. The slide show will be shown on a screen in the foyer of the gym and will be operated using a touch screen.

a) Create the home slide with links to slides for each activity.

b) Design a master slide to be used to create a slide for each activity. There should be a link to the home slide.

c) Using the master slide, create a slide for each activity. On each slide there should be:

   i. A picture related to the activity.

   ii. Some text describing the activity.

   iii. A link to a website with more information about the activity.

   iv. The date last edited in the footer.

d) Provide evidence that you have done this.

Answer

The answer to this question is a presentation that meets the specification. The slide show would be expected to be colourful and attractive, and have simple navigation centred on the home slide with a link back to it from every other slide. The slides for each activity should all have a picture, text, a link to a website and the date last edited in the footer.

> **TOP TIP** ✓
>
> A good way to test the slide show would be to run it using an interactive whiteboard.

> **TOP TIP** ✓
>
> In an examination, evidence that you have done this would be a word processed document with screen shots of each slide with an explanation of what you have done.

1. Which of these would **not** be linked to from a presentation?

    A   website

    B   word processing document

    C   video file

    D   fax   *(1 mark)*

2. Which of these would **not** be used for a presentation?

    A   monitor screen

    B   scanner

    C   multimedia projector

    D   mouse   *(1 mark)*

3. All the slides in a presentation are printed to give to the audience. Which setting would be used?

    A   Full Page Slides

    B   Notes Pages

    C   6 Slides Horizontal

    D   Print Current Slide   *(1 mark)*

4. Prepare a presentation about security.

    a) Choose a slide layout, theme, colour scheme and animation scheme.   *(3 marks)*

    b) The first slide should introduce the topic to your audience.   *(1 mark)*

    c) Next, slides should prompt you to explain:

        i.   Why security is a concern.   *(1 mark)*

        ii. The different threats from the Internet and how to counter them.   *(3 marks)*

    d) Put the date and your name on every slide.   *(2 marks)*

    e) Save and print your work showing six slides on one page.   *(1 mark)*

TOP TIP

Look at how many marks there are for each question. You should name and explain at least that many different threats from the Internet.

Chapter 9: Communications, networks, the Internet and email

> **You need to know:**
>
> - A **local area network (LAN)** is a collection of connected computers in a small geographical area.
> - **Wide area networks (WAN)** connect computers across large geographical areas.
> - The **Internet** is a network of networks and connects computers around the world.
> - An **Internet Service Provider (ISP)** connects subscribers' computers to the Internet.
> - To communicate over the **Internet**, computers use **TCP/IP (Transfer Control Protocol/Internet Protocol)**.
> - The **World Wide Web** consists of millions of **web pages.** You view these using a **browser**.
> - **Services** available on the Web are: search engines; email; news groups; forums, chatrooms and instant messaging; uploading and downloading digital media, e.g. music, images and video; social networking.
> - **Web 2.0** facilitates creativity, collaboration and sharing between users.
> - An **intranet** provides many of the features of the Internet for use within an organisation.
> - A **VPN** (Virtual Private Network) provides especially secure remote access to an intranet.
> - **Threats** from the Internet include: spam; viruses; phishing; pharming; adware; access to inappropriate information; cookies; and hacking. Ways to prevent these include: spam filters, antivirus software, pop-up blockers, parental control or filter software, and usernames and passwords.

Networks

A **network** is two or more connected computers that can share resources and communicate.

Local area network (LAN)

A **LAN**:

- Connects computers across a small to medium-sized geographical area, e.g. an office, school or campus.
- Shares resources, e.g. hardware and data.
- Enables communication between computers connected to it, e.g. using instant messaging.
- Is administered centrally.

Most LANs are **client/server** networks. **Client** computers (or network stations) are the computers connected to the network. Clients communicate with each other through the server. The **server** has a faster processor, more RAM and more backing storage than client computers. A large LAN may have several servers. For instance, a **file server** may look after the organisation of the files on the network; a **database server** hosts a database management system and a database on the network.

A **peer-to-peer LAN** does not use a server. Every computer communicates directly with the other computers on the network. Because of performance limitations, it is limited to small networks of fewer than 10 computers.

Advantages

- The cost of software licences could be less as they may only be needed for the average number of concurrent users, not for every computer.

- Shared hardware can be better quality at a lower cost per user, e.g. a network printer.

- Shared data allows more effective collaborative working, e.g. users can work on a single shared document.

- Users' access rights can be administered centrally, e.g. the marketing staff can access their own files, but not the files of the human resources staff.

- The network can be maintained from any network station, e.g. if a password has been forgotten, it can be reset.

- Security can be administered centrally, e.g. automatic backups and virus protection.

Disadvantages

- The initial set-up costs can be higher because a server and network cabling are needed.

- Viruses are more easily spread across networks.

Cabled and wireless network connections

Cables can be used to connect all the components of a LAN. A computer is connected to a cabled LAN by connecting a network cable from the computer's **network interface card (NIC)** to a network **hub** or **switch**, which in turn is connected to the other devices, hubs and switches that constitute the network. A gateway connects networks and provides access from one network to another, e.g. a modem is a gateway that connects a home network to the Internet.

A **wireless LAN (WLAN)** consists of:

- **Wireless NICs** in each computer.

- **Wireless access points** which broadcast to and receive signals from wireless NICs. These are usually connected to a cabled network.

- **Routers** which enable several computers to communicate at the same time through a wireless access point.

WLANs are slower than cabled LANs and are used where it is impractical to use a cabled LAN, e.g. in the home. The range of a WLAN can be limited, e.g. because of impenetrable walls. The range can be extended using a more up-to-date wireless router or a wireless signal **booster**.

> **TOP TIP** ✓
> Encryption is encoding data so that it cannot be understood by someone who does not have the encryption key.

Connection to a WLAN is limited to authorised users by a **WEP** (Wired Equivalent Privacy) key, which must be entered before connection. WEP encrypts data on the network, but has been superseded by **WPA** (Wi-Fi Protected Access), which provides stronger encryption.

Figure 9.1 *A bluetooth enabled watch that connects to your smartphone*

Wireless access points are installed in public places, e.g. railways stations, enabling widespread access to the Internet.

Wide area network (WAN)

A WAN connects computers across a large geographical area, e.g. a city or internationally. Information is transmitted in many ways; e.g. using fibre optic cables and satellites.

Bluetooth

Bluetooth is a form of wireless communication designed to enable devices that are within 10 meters of each other, e.g. a laptop and a smartphone, to communicate. Data is transferred at a rate of 720 Kbps.

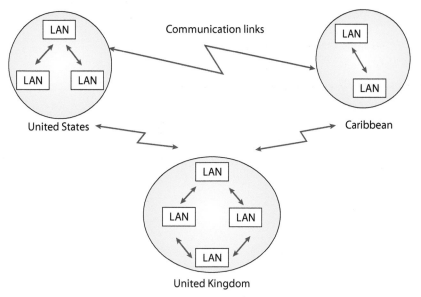

Figure 9.2 *A wide area network (WAN)*

The Internet

The **Internet** consists of many linked but independently maintained and administered networks. Each network on the Internet is responsible for formulating its own policies, procedures and rules.

To connect to the Internet using a PC, you need an **Internet Service Provider (ISP)**. You also need a **web browser**, email and other software that allows you to use the services and facilities available on the Internet; and a **modem** (**mo**dulator/**dem**odulator) which converts the digital signals from a computer into analogue signals that can be transmitted over a telephone line.

Bandwidth is the volume of data that can be transmitted over a network connection.

- **Narrowband** users **dial up** their ISP using a telephone. Data is transmitted at speeds up to 56 Kbps. This is slow but inexpensive.

- **Broadband** is data transmission using:

  - **ADSL** (Asymmetric Digital Subscriber Line), which provides speeds up to 100Mbps and a continuous connection to the Internet;

  - **cable** technology;

  - **mobile telephone networks**, e.g. 3G.

> Each computer on the Internet has a unique **IP (Internet Protocol)** address, e.g. 196.161.232.4. The IP address could be **static** (it remains the same every time you connect) or it could be **dynamic** (it changes each time you connect).

> **TCP/IP (Transmission Control Protocol/Internet Protocol)** is a set of rules used on the Internet to define how computers communicate with each other. It is a universal standard that enables hardware and different operating systems to communicate.

World Wide Web

The **World Wide Web** (or the Web) is a collection of multimedia services that run on the Internet.

> **TOP TIP** ✔
> The Internet and the Web are not the same. The Internet is the network and the Web is the multimedia services that run on it.

Browser

A **web browser**, e.g. Google Chrome, is software that lets you access web pages stored on **web servers** and download files, e.g. programs and video.

Figure 9.3 *A web page accessed using the Microsoft Internet Explorer browser*

Web address or URL (Uniform Resource Locator)

IP addresses (e.g. 202.168.3.34) are difficult for people to remember so web addresses are used instead, e.g. http://www.edexcel.com/quals/Pages/default.aspx

http://	The type of resource the address refers to is a web page.
www.edexcel.com	The web server is called www.edexcel and it is run by an international commercial organisation.
/quals/Pages/	On the web server, the file that will be displayed is in the directory called *quals* in a subdirectory called *Pages*.
default.aspx	The file is called default. The extension indicates the type of file. Here, .aspx indicates that it is a .NET Web form.

Services accessible on the Web

You can:

- View web pages.
- Use a search engine.
- Send and receive email.
- Upload and download digital media, e.g. music.
- Share images with friends and family.
- Use online shopping and banking.
- Download software, e.g. Apps.
- Use **social networking** to communicate with family and friends.
- **Chat** online in chatrooms or using IM (Instant Messaging).
- Publish an online personal diary (or **blog**) with narrative, pictures and hyperlinks.
- Access information and join discussions, e.g. using **newsgroup**s and **forums**.
- Watch TV and listen to the radio.
- Access customer support, e.g. FAQs or download a service guide for a printer.
- Build your own website.

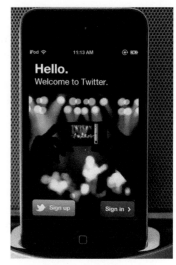

Figure 9.4 *Using Twitter for social networking*

Finding information on the Web

You can search for and access information by:

- **Surfing**: navigate by clicking on hyperlinks, enter a web address or use a search engine.
- Using a **directory**, e.g. Yahoo! Directory shows a list of broad categories available, e.g. Arts and Humanities, broken down into subcategories. When you select a category, a list of subcategories is displayed. You select deeper and deeper until you find the information you want.
- Using a **search engine**, e.g. www.google.co.uk. Type in the address or use the search facilities built into the browser, then enter keywords.
- Using a **web bot**. Bot is short for **robot**, and a web bot is software that can run automatically on the Web for searching and alerting you to items of interest.

Intranet

- An **intranet** is a local version of the Internet used within an organisation. Intranets provide many of the services available over the Internet, e.g. email, chat, websites and search, but only for authorised users within the organisation.
- If an organisation has an intranet and allows secure access by people working off site, e.g. at home, it is referred to as an **extranet.**

A **VPN (Virtual Private Network)** is a private, secure connection that runs across the Internet. Its purpose is similar to an extranet but network traffic will be encrypted and Internet protocols such as TCP/IP may not be used. It can be thought of as a separate 'pipe' inside the Internet.

Electronic mail (email)

Using **email** you can send electronic messages to an individual or contact group, and receive messages from others.

Sending email is free (provided you already have the hardware and software and Internet access), is much faster than mail delivered by post, and you can send as many emails as you like at any time.

To access your email, you can use:

- **Webmail**, e.g Hotmail. This runs within a browser and you log on to a website to retrieve your email. Access to email is slower than using an email client and there is a more restricted range of features,

- An **email client**, e.g. Microsoft Outlook, is software that runs on your computer and enables you to send and receive email. An email client tends to run more quickly than webmail and it will have a wider range of customisable options, but it has to be installed and can be more complex to use.

Sending email

To create a new email message in Microsoft Outlook, with the **Inbox** open on screen, click on the **New** button in the toolbar.

- In the **To...** field, enter the email address of the person you are sending it to, or click on the **To...** field and select an address from the **Contacts**.

- In the **Cc...** field, enter the addresses of people the email will be copied to.

- If you want to send a copy of the email to someone and want to hide this from the other recipients, enter their email address in the **Bcc...** field.

- In the **Subject** field, enter a phrase that describes what your email is about.

- Enter your message.

- **Attach** any files to be sent with the email, e.g. a spreadsheet file.

- Press **Send** and your email is placed in the **Outbox**.

- If you have a permanent connection to the Internet, the message will automatically be sent. Otherwise click on the **Send/Receive** button in the toolbar.

Receiving and replying to an email message

Open Microsoft Outlook. Click on the **Send/ Receive** button in the toolbar. The email software connects to the email server and downloads your email into the **Inbox.** If you have a permanent connection to the Internet, this happens automatically and you will be alerted by a sound when an email arrives.

You could:

- Read your email.

- Open or save an attachment.

- Click on **Reply** and a new message opens which is addressed to the person who sent you the email.

- Click on **Forward** and a new email opens which includes the current message and attachments.

- **Delete** the email.

Storing email messages

Microsoft Outlook sets up folders to store email messages:

- **Inbox.** As emails are received, they are put in the Inbox.

- **Drafts.** Emails you are working on are saved in this folder.

- **Sent Items.** When email is sent, a copy is placed in this folder.

- **Deleted Items.** Deleted emails are saved in this folder.

- **Outbox.** Email that is ready to send is stored in the Outbox.

- **'Personal'.** If you need to save email you have received, you can create your own personal folders.

Contacts

Contacts store information such as email address, full name and postal address. You can set up a group of contacts and send an email to everyone in the **Contact Group** at the same time.

Online shopping

You can order goods online and pay for them using a credit or debit card. The goods are delivered by post to the address you specify.

Online shopping can be convenient:

- You can do your shopping at any time.

- You do not have to leave your home.

- A wider range of goods is available.

- Specialist goods, which are not on sale locally, are available.

- It is easier to compare prices and availability from different suppliers.

Figure 9.5 *Online shopping*

But there are risks:

- You cannot inspect the goods other than on screen.

- If the goods are not satisfactory, you have to post them back and claim a refund.

- If you do not have a debit or credit card you cannot shop online.

- There is a risk of online fraud.

Internet banking

Many bank accounts can be accessed over the Internet. You do not need to visit a branch and some banks have no branches, e.g. First Direct. Internet banking can have lower charges because the cost to the bank of providing the service is much less.

Mailing lists, newsgroups, chatrooms and instant messaging (IM)

Mailing lists, newsgroups, chatrooms and instant messaging (IM) enable a group of people with common interests to communicate with each other:

- A **mailing list** uses email. Members send and receive messages from the list. Not all groups are open to everyone.

- A subscriber to a **newsgroup** logs on and **posts** a message. When other subscribers log on, they can read the message and reply. A subscriber can look at a **thread** of related messages.

- A **chatroom** is a group of people communicating with one another interactively in real time. Some chatrooms discuss specific topics, but many chatrooms cover a range of subjects.

- **Instant messaging** enables you to chat privately with another person. Messages are sent immediately.

Video conferencing

Video conferencing enables users to see and speak to each other at a distance, e.g. using Skype. It can be one to one or involve several people communicating at the same time. Video camera systems can be simple webcams or may be able to zoom in and out. The display could be on one or more monitors or a large screen.

Web 2.0

Web 2.0 describes a trend towards collaboration and sharing between web users. These web services are associated with Web 2.0:

- **Social networking** where you can interact with a circle of friends, those with similar interests or a wider community, e.g. **Facebook**.

- **YouTube** enables members to upload videos and allows anyone to view and comment on them.

- **Worldisround** encourages world travellers to upload and share pictures and add commentary to make a record of their experiences for friends and family at home.

- **iTunes** and **Spotify** sell digital music which can be downloaded. Users can organise and browse their music collections.

- **Blogs** are online diaries with narrative, pictures and hyperlinks. Anyone can set up a blog on almost any topic, e.g. hollywoodlife.com is a celebrity news blog.

- **Wikis** enable you to describe and comment on topics in collaboration with other web users, e.g. **Wikipedia** is an online encyclopedia. Anyone can contribute but this is moderated so that what is available is often written by experts.

Internet security

There are many threats from the Internet.

Threat	Protection
Hacking is **unauthorised access** to your computer or files and to your personal information, e.g. email and bank accounts.	Use **a username and password.** Don't give these to anyone and don't write them down.
	Use a **firewall.** This is a combination of hardware and software that controls network traffic between a secure computer or network and the Internet.
	Use **WEP** (Wired Equivalent Privacy) or **WPA** (Wi-Fi Protected Access) codes which prevent unauthorised connection to a wireless network.

Threat	Protection
	Encrypt data. Encrypted data cannot be understood by someone without the encryption key. This prevents hackers understanding data on the ICT systems they access.
	Use a transaction log to track use of the system. This can show hackers' activities and help identify them.
	Hacking is often by authorised users accessing ICT systems they should not. Restrict users' file access rights to prevent this.
Spam is unsolicited email. There is so much spam that it can swamp legitimate email.	Use a **spam filter** to scan incoming email and remove unwanted email messages.
A **virus** is malicious software installed on a computer without the user's consent. Viruses can be attached to emails and downloaded with software.	Use **antivirus** software which checks for viruses and removes them, e.g. McAfee VirusScan. Treat files from unknown sources with caution.
Phishing is an attempt to find out personal information in order to carry out identity theft and fraud, e.g. you receive an email asking you to access your online bank by clicking on a hyperlink in the email. However, the link takes you to a fraudulent website where you enter your username and password. These are stolen and used to take money from your bank account.	Look for spelling and grammar errors, which are unlikely in an email from a bank. Suspect a phishing attack when you receive an email claiming to be from a bank, as they do not usually send unsolicited emails. Check that you have an account with the bank. If you are worried your bank is really trying to contact you, break the connection with the email then contact the bank directly. Remember that you are unlikely to win a competition you haven't entered!
Pharming is an attempt to collect personal information when users connect to legitimate websites. **Spyware** installed on a user's computer logs their personal information as they enter it.	Detect and destroy spyware using antivirus software and specialised programs, e.g. Spybot Search & Destroy.
Adware is unsolicited advertising which often generates **pop-up** adverts.	Block adware and pop-ups in a browser or using antivirus software and specialised programs, e.g. Spybot Search & Destroy.
Access to inappropriate information, e.g. children accessing pornography.	Use **parental control (or filter) software** to restrict children's access to inappropriate information, e.g. CYBERsitter. Features are: Access to some web addresses, searches on some keywords and sending some personal information are blocked. The URLs visited are recorded. Parents are notified by email that blocking is occurring. Parents are able to change filter settings over the Internet.
Cookies are saved on your hard disk by websites and contain personal information that can be accessed by the website.	Use a **cookie manager** to block cookies or remove them using a browser.

```
27 March 2013

Dear Brinton's Bank User,

We recently have determined that your Brinton's Bank account, needs to
be updated again. This update will help us in making our database more
secure. This procedure has become the standard and must follow way for
any Bank providing Online Banking services. activity. This new security
statement will helps us continue to offer Brinton's Bank as a secure
Online Banking Service. We appreciate your cooperation and assistance.

Please click on continue, to the verification process and ensure your
Account information is entered correctly to get verified.
Continue to Internet Banking
http://www.navyhovik.no/images/kaz/www/brintonsbank.com/customer.ibc/
online/banking/Update/brintonbank%20online%20-%20Welcome.index.htm


Sincerely,
Brinton's Bank Online Account Security.

_____


Brinton's Bank plc and Brinton's Bank Scotland plc are authorised and
regulated by the Financial Services Authority and signatories to the
Banking Codes. FSA authorization can be checked on the FSA's Register at
www.fsa.gov.uk/register. Brinton's Bank plc and Brinton's Bank Scotland
plc are members of the Financial Services Compensation Scheme and the
Financial Ombudsman Service. Brinton's Bank plc.
```

Figure 9.6 *A phishing email*

What you see on the Web is not always what it seems. To be **safe and sure** that information is reliable, you should always ask yourself:

- Can I trust the source of the information?

- Is the evidence from a primary source or are they reporting someone else's account?

- Is the source sufficiently knowledgeable?

- Is the information likely to be biased or unreliable in some way? Why?

- Why am I being asked for personal information?

- Will providing this information put me at risk?

Worked Example

Julie has a dog called Fido. At work she logs on to the company network. Her password is Fido.

a) Explain why using Fido as a password is not good security.

b) Give an example of a stronger password and explain why it is stronger.

c) Describe two precautions Julie should take to protect her password.

Answers

a) Fido is not a strong password as it could easily be guessed by someone who knows Julie.

b) F2i8D67o would be a stronger password because: it includes upper case and lower case alphabetic characters and numbers; and it is much longer.

c) Julie should not tell anyone else her password and she should not write it down.

1. A company has four workstations linked by network cables to a server. What type of network is this?

   A   client/server

   B   extranet

   C   WAN

   D   wireless LAN   *(1 mark)*

2. What could parents use to prevent their children accessing inappropriate websites?

   A   spam filter

   B   cookies

   C   filter software

   D   antivirus software   *(1 mark)*

3. A company has an intranet. Which of these statements must be true?

   A   Employees can access the intranet from home.

   B   At work, employees cannot send email to other employees.

   C   An intranet must include Internet access.

   D   Employees can access the intranet at work.
                                              (1 mark)

4. What information is needed to connect to a wireless network?

   A   URL

   B   WEP or WPA key

   C   fax number

   D   email address   *(1 mark)*

5. Which of the following statements is **not** an advantage of using a LAN?

   A   sharing data

   B   viruses are spread more easily

   C   software licensing can be less expensive

   D   instant messaging   *(1 mark)*

6. You receive an email asking you to connect to an online bank by clicking on a link in the email. What could you do to protect yourself from this phishing attack?   *(2 marks)*

7. A home network provides Internet access for two laptops and a desktop PC.

   a)   What is needed so that all of these can connect to the Internet?   *(4 marks)*

   b)   Describe **two** benefits of a home network.
                                              (2 marks)

   TOP TIP
   Describe two very different benefits.

   c)   A mobile phone can connect to the home network. Why would this be done?   *(2 marks)*

8. A search engine is used to find information on the Web.

   a)   Describe how you would use a search engine to find information.   *(1 mark)*

   b)   Describe another way to find information on the Web.   *(1 mark)*

9. Describe **two** ways of communicating online while you are using a computer.   *(2 marks)*

10. Discuss the advantages and disadvantages of online shopping.   *(4 marks)*

   TOP TIP
   Give examples to illustrate each point you make.

Chapter 9: Communications, networks, the Internet and email

Chapter 10: Web authoring

> **You need to know:**
>
> - You **publish** a website by creating linked web pages and uploading them to a web server.
> - You can create web pages using:
>   - **application software**
>   - **a text editor**
>   - **web authoring software**.
> - You can include the following features on web pages: **text, images, backgrounds, links to other web pages, links within the web page, email links, tables** and **styles**.
> - Web pages are usually written in **Hypertext Markup Language (HTML)** and should have filenames that end in .htm or .html, be lower case, and have no spaces in them.
> - You promote your website by **submitting its web address to search engines** and using **meta tags.**

Creating and publishing a website

Creating web pages using applications software

- You can **create a web page** by saving a word processor document as an HTML file. In Microsoft Word, click the **File** tab and select **Save As** and set **Save as type** to **Web Page (*.htm; *.html).**

- You can **insert links** to other web pages: on the **Insert** tab select **Hyperlink.**

- Other applications have similar features, e.g. Excel.

Creating web pages by writing HTML using a text editor

You can create web pages by writing HTML in a **text editor**, e.g. WordPad. These can be viewed in a browser, e.g. Firefox.

> **HTML structure**
>
> The HTML for a web page starts with the <html> tag and ends with the </html> tag
>
> The first section is the header which starts with <head> and ends with </head>
>
> The next section is the body which starts with <body> and ends with </body>
>
> Each section includes different tags or pairs of tags:
>
> The header section can include these tags:
>
> **<title>My building company</title>**
>
> Whatever is between the <title> tags will appear in the browser's title bar.
>
> The body section can include these tags:
>
> **<h1>We build houses</h1>**
>
> These are heading tags. <h2> headings have slightly smaller text, and <h3> headings have even smaller text.

> ### `<img src="images/ahousewebuilt.jpg">`
>
> This tag inserts a picture. The picture file ahousewebuilt.jpg is saved in the images folder in the same folder as the web page.
>
> ### `<p>The house we built is made of stone. </p>`
>
> The `<p>` tags indicate a paragraph of text.
>
> ### `<a href ="http://www.hud.ac.uk" >The University of Huddersfield</a>`
>
> inserts a hyperlink to a web page.
>
> The tags can be modified to achieve different effects:
>
> ### `<body bgcolor ="blue" >`
>
> makes the background colour of the web page blue;
>
> ### `<body background="images/ahousewebuilt.jpg" >`
>
> makes the picture in the jpg file the background;
>
> ### `<font size="5" color="red" face="Arial" </font>`
>
> sets the size of the text, its colour, and the typeface.

Web authoring software

Web authoring software, e.g. Adobe Dreamweaver, allows you to write web pages both as they appear on screen (**Design View**) and in HTML (**Code View**), and provides tools for managing your website.

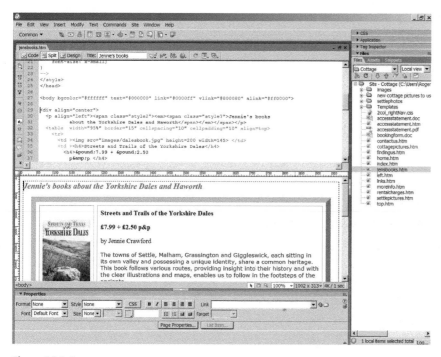

Figure 10.1 *Dreamweaver*

Creating a website

You begin by setting up a new website: in the **Site** menu select **New Site.** Enter the **Site Name**; the **Local Root Folder**, that is, the folder on the hard disk where the files will be saved; and the **Default Images Folder**, e.g. images.

Creating a web page

To create a new web page, in the **File** menu select **New**.

On the **General** tab choose a template by selecting a category and page design.

Click on **Create** and the new page is displayed. You replace the dummy text with your own.

Save your new page, and this will appear in the **Files** tab in the **Site Panel**. This shows all the pages and other resources used in your website.

In **Design View**, you can type in text. In the **Text** menu, you can change the **Font, Size** and **Color.**

To **insert an image** in a web page, find the picture in the images folder in the **Site Panel**, and in **Design View** drag it across on to the web page.

Alt text

Alternate (ALT) text associates a text description with an image. The text is downloaded and displayed on the web page before the image, and when you hover the cursor over the image, the text is displayed. The advantages of using ALT text are:

- Partially sighted people can use voice synthesis software that reads the ALT text to them.

- Web pages are more likely to be fully indexed by search engines as web spiders recognise the content of text but not images.

To associate ALT text with a picture, in **Design View**, select the image and in the **Properties** panel, type in the text in the **ALT** box.

Background

To set a **background colour**, in the **Modify** menu, select **Page Properties** and choose a background colour.

To set a **background image,** in the **Modify** menu, select **Page Properties.** Browse to find a background image.

Links

To insert a **text link** to another web page, in **Design View** in the **Insert** menu, select **Hyperlink** or in **Code View**, enter **<a href="http://www. google. co.uk">Google</a>** in the body section, for example.

To insert a **graphic link** to another web page, in **Design View**, insert the image, highlight it and enter the full web address of the web page to link to in the **Properties** panel in the **Link** box.

> **TOP TIP** ✔
>
> **Spambots** search web pages and collect email addresses where **mailto:** has been used. You can reduce spam by inserting your email address as an image.

Links within a page are useful for navigating within large pages. For example, this code in the web page **glossary.html** makes the text '**Top**' a hyperlink to a jump point called **TopOfPage** in the same web page:

```
<a href="glossary.html#TopOfPage"> Top</a>
```

Clicking on 'Top' navigates to the jump point marked by the code:

```
<a name="TopOfPage"></a>
```

To insert an email link, in the **Insert** menu select **Email Link.** Alternatively, in **Code View**, enter:

```
<ahref="mailto:customerservices@pearsoned.com">Contact Customer Services</a>
```

The text displayed is <u>Contact Customer Services</u> and this opens an email that is automatically addressed to **customerservices@pearsoned.com.**

Tables

Tables help with the layout of a web page, because the position of text and images is easily controlled by inserting them in the cells of the table. To insert a table in **Design View**, position the cursor where the table is to be placed. In the **Insert** menu, select **Table.**

Styles

Styles control the appearance of text and can help with consistency.

Inline style declarations affect only the text in the tag, e.g. for red text on a silver background in a particular <h2> heading, insert this code:

> **<h2 style="color: red; background-color: silver">write your heading text here</ h2>**

Embedded style declarations affect all the same tags within a web page. For example, to ensure that all <h2> headings in a web page are blue, insert this code in the header section:

> **<style> h2 {color: blue} </style>**

External **stylesheets** are used to create a consistent appearance over several web pages. To do this, set up an external stylesheet and link your web pages to it.

Set up an external stylesheet by creating a text file called, e.g. **style.css**, with these or similar statements in it, and save this in the same folder as the web pages that will use it.

> **h2 {color: red}**
>
> **p {font-family:Arial; font-size: 20; background-color: cyan; color: white}**

Link every web page in your website to the external stylesheet by inserting this code in the header section:

> **<link rel="stylesheet" type="text/css" href = "style.css">**

TOP TIP ✔

Cascading Stylesheets (CSS) means an inline style declaration overrides an embedded style declaration and both override an external stylesheet.

TOP TIP ✔

Make sure that your home page is named **index.html** and all filenames are in lower case with no spaces and use the **.html** extension.

Uploading a website

You have to copy your website to a web server before it is available over the Internet. Many Internet Service Providers (ISPs) offer hosting on their web servers and the tools to move your website from your hard disk to their web server.

Promoting a website

You can help search engines find your website by:

- Submitting your website to search engines; e.g. to submit the address of your website to multiple search engines you can use http://www.addpro.com/submit30.htm.

- Using meta tags; e.g. this tag goes in the header section and provides a short description that is displayed when you point at search results:

> **<meta name="description" content="Hazel Cottage for holidays in Settle, Yorkshire">**

a) Create a web page advertising tourism in the Yorkshire Dales, UK.

The web page is based on the design below and you should create the required content.

Provide evidence of your work in a word processed document.

Logo	Page title
Links to: A search engine At least three websites about the Yorkshire Dales	Page content – text and at least one image
Contact details	

b) Identify the software you used to create and run the web page.

c) Explain how you avoided copyright restrictions on:

   i. the logo

   ii. the image.

d) Take a screen shot of the web page running in a browser and include this in the word processed document.

e) Evaluate your work.

Answer

In the word processed document:

a) The web page I created is shown in Figure 10.2.

b) Dreamweaver was used to create the web page, which is shown running in the Firefox browser.

c) I avoided copyright restrictions in this way:

   i. I downloaded the logo from www.clker.com/ clipart-3439.html. It is public domain clip art.

   ii. The image is a photograph I took on holiday.

d) See Figure 10.2.

e) Evaluation:

- For a real web page you would need to construct an original logo.

- All the links were tested and all of them work.

- I divided the cell containing the content into two cells so that I could control the layout of the image and the text.

- The layout and content meet requirements but the appearance could be improved.

Figure 10.2 *The web page I created*

1. Which of the following is applications software?

    A   Operating system

    B   HTML

    C   BIOS

    D   Web authoring   *(1 mark)*

2. Which of these services is NOT usually provided by an ISP?

    A   Connection to the Internet

    B   Website hosting

    C   Email

    D   Website promotion   *(1 mark)*

3. Which of the following software could NOT be used to generate HTML?

    A   Word processor, e.g. Word

    B   Spreadsheet, e.g. Excel

    C   Graphics, e.g. Photoshop

    D   Web authoring, e.g. Dreamweaver *(1 mark)*

4. Build a website that provides information about activities in your neighbourhood. Use web authoring software.

a) Plan the website by drawing a structure diagram and sketching the layout of each of the pages.

    i.   Use a table to layout the home page.
                                        (1 mark)

    ii. There should be graphic links from the home page to pages about at least two activities.   *(2 marks)*

    iii. Each activity page should include images and text in a variety of fonts, colours and sizes, and a link back to the home page.
                                        (2 marks)

TOP TIP

To demonstrate you have selected different fonts, colours and sizes, do not use the default settings.

b) Create the website you have planned. You should provide evidence you have done this in a word processed file, which includes a screenshot of each web page running in a browser.   *(5 marks)*

Chapter 11: Data input and output

Data collection and input

Data capture form

Data can be collected by writing on a **data capture form**, e.g. a printed questionnaire. The data is subsequently input to the computer by typing it in using a keyboard and the data is saved on a hard disk (**key-to-disk**).

When designing a questionnaire you should:

- Collect the information in a way that assists computer input, e.g. use tick boxes and codes to make filling in the form and data entry easier and faster.
- Lay out the form in a straightforward way.
- Clearly state why the information is being collected.
- Use simple language that is easily understood.
- Say clearly what information must be provided and what is optional.
- Provide help in answering, if necessary.
- Provide enough space for the answer.
- Collect all the information needed, but no more.
- Avoid asking questions that may not be answered truthfully.
- Request the information in an intuitively logical order, e.g. name and address.
- Encourage people to write their name clearly, and to sign and date the form.
- Allow people who fill in the form to give you their preferred contact details, e.g. address, telephone number or email address.
- Make it easy for people who fill in the form to submit it, e.g. give the name and address of the person the form is to be returned to on the form.
- Use codes to make filling in the form and data entry easier.

Codes

Codes are shorthand for more detailed and lengthy information, e.g. DOB means date of birth. Codes reduce mistakes; make data entry, verification and validation faster and easier; reduce the amount of storage space required; and make output more concise.

Direct data entry (DDE)

DDE allows data to be entered directly into the computer, saving the time, expense and effort of key-to-disk. DDE methods include:

- Input screens or online forms.
- Optical Mark Reader (OMR) forms.
- Optical Character Recognition (OCR).
- Magnetic stripe card readers.
- Chip and PIN card readers.
- Bar code readers.
- Radio frequency identification (RFID).
- Sensors.

Verification and validation

Verification ensures that the data written on a printed form is entered into a computer accurately:

Visual verification – a person types in the data from the form then checks that the data displayed on the monitor screen is the same as that written on the form, and corrects errors.

Double-entry verification has three steps:

1. The data is typed into the computer and saved as version 1.
2. Someone else types the data into the computer and saves it as version 2.
3. The computer compares version 1 and version 2. If they are not the same, a mistake has been made and this is corrected.

Validation checks help ensure that data is reasonable:

- **Range check** – ensures data is in a sensible range.
- **Presence check** – ensures data that is required is entered.
- **Type checks** – ensures data is of a type that is expected.
- **Length check** – ensures the number of characters entered is less than the maximum.

Limitations of verification and validation

Even after thorough verification and validation checks, we cannot be certain that data is entirely correct. These checks do not always discover if someone has entered the wrong information, e.g. if your name is 'Allan' and you mistakenly enter 'Alan' in an online form, a validation check would not identify this error.

TOP TIP
Verification ensures that data is accurately input into a computer. Validation ensures that data input to a computer is reasonable.

Output is dependent on the availability of the data it is derived from. If this is not available when output is requested, then it cannot be produced.

Output design and delivery tips

- Keep the layout, navigation and language simple.

- Include titles or introductory sentences where necessary.

- Tailor the output to the needs of the audience.

- Ensure information is easy to find and make sure it's in a logical order.

- Provide necessary information, but also provide analysis or calculation if needed.

- Use tables, charts and graphs to summarise, and graphics that relate to the information.

- Provide links or appendices with further information if needed.

- Indicate the source of the information and state the time and date the output was last updated.

- Output should be up to date and produced as soon as possible, especially if it has limited usefulness or data changes quickly.

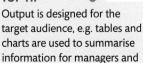

TOP TIP
Output is designed for the target audience, e.g. tables and charts are used to summarise information for managers and strategic decision makers.

TOP TIP
Be clear when you should use a pie chart, bar chart or line chart. Examiners expect A* students to answer correctly questions that many other students get wrong.

Tables and charts

- **Tables** are often produced in spreadsheets and exported to other applications. A table is a straightforward way of summarising information; however, it does not help us interpret it.

- A **pie chart** summarises information about the relative importance of different categories.

- A **bar chart** or **column chart** is used when either the vertical or horizontal scale is in categories, e.g. different colours of cars in a car park. It is more complex than a pie chart and provides more information.

- A **line chart** is used when the information on the horizontal scale is continuous.

Characteristics of the output device

The **characteristics of the output device** affect the layout of the output, e.g. credit card readers have a small receipt printer so that the **layout** of receipts focuses more on providing the information customers need rather than attractive design.

- Printed output may be better in either **landscape** or **portrait orientation**. A **printer spacing chart** is used to design the layout.

- Much less information can be output on the screen of a smart phone than on a 19″ monitor. Screen output can be designed using a **screen spacing chart**, which is similar to a printer spacing chart.

Accessibility of output

Accessibility could be affected by:

- **Connection speed** – a slow Internet connection could constrain access, e.g. web pages with features that require 20Mb broadband may load too slowly on a smart phone with 2Mb Internet access.

- **Usage limit** – if you exceed the usage limit on your smart phone or home broadband you are likely to be surcharged or blocked.

- **Physical access** – some people do not have immediate physical access to computers and smart phones. This restricts their opportunities to use the Web.

- **Disability** – particular care needs to be taken to ensure people with disabilities, e.g. people with restricted vision or hearing, or the physically disabled, can access output.

TOP TIP ✓
www.w3.org has design guidelines for improving accessibility.

Worked Example

Data capture forms are used to input data.

The data on the form is input by typing it into a computer.

a) Describe one method of verification.

b) Describe two validation checks that could be carried out on the Name.

c) Dates are input in dd/mm/yyyy format.

    i. How would the dates entered need to be adapted so that validation is successful?

    ii. How could the form be modified to reduce errors in dates?

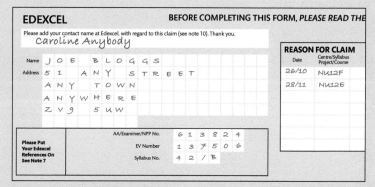

Figure 11.1 *Part of a data capture form used by Edexcel*

Answers

a) The data could be visually verified by checking that what is shown on the screen after input is the same as the data written on the form.

b) The Name could be checked to make sure it is no longer than 19 characters and that all the characters are alphabetic.

c) Dates.

    i. The year has been left off and could be added when the data is typed in so that rejects are avoided.

    ii. The form could be modified so that dates are entered in clearly labelled boxes, e.g.:

D	D	/	M	M	/	2	0	Y	Y
2	6	/	1	0	/	2	0	1	2
2	8	/	1	1	/	2	0	1	2

1. A railway company uses a two-letter code to record where trains are going, e.g. VE means the train is going to Venice, MA to Manchester, LA to Lausanne and PA to Paris. Which code would **not** pass the validation check?

   A LA

   B MA

   C VE

   D P7   *(1 mark)*

2. Which input method is not DDE?

   A pressure sensor

   B RFID

   C swipe card reader

   D entering written information using a keyboard   *(1 mark)*

3. Last year a car showroom sold 5000 cars: 1500 were blue; 500 red; 2000 black; and 1000 other colours.

   a) Name a type of chart that would clearly show that black is the most popular colour and create this chart.   *(1 mark)*

   b) Explain why a line graph would not be appropriate.   *(2 marks)*

4. A website gives the exchange rate between Pounds Sterling and the Euro. It is updated each month. Explain why exporters might prefer a website that was updated more frequently.   *(1 mark)*

5. Parents who want to take their very young children to an art club have to fill in an online application form.

   a) Design an online application form.   *(9 marks)*

   TOP TIP
   Go beyond the obvious. If you were running the art club, what might you need to know?

   b) Most parents get the club receptionist to fill in the form for them at the art club. They could write the information on a printed form. Would this be more appropriate? Explain your answer.
                                              (3 marks)

Chapter 12: Applications and effects of ICT

ICT systems

Payroll

Every company or business has to pay its employees. An example of a payroll system is shown in Figure 12.1.

- Employees each have their own swipe card and their unique employee number is recorded on it. The amount of hours they work is recorded on the swipe card by recording when they arrive (*clock in*) and when they leave (*clock out*). All this information is **input** into the ICT system each day.

> **TOP TIP** ✓
> Validation checks help ensure that data is reasonable.

- **Validation** checks are made on all the data input and the validated data is written to the **unsorted transaction file.** Data that does not change every week is saved on the **old master file.**

- The **payroll program** matches an employee's **transaction file record** with the corresponding **old master file record**. The hours worked are calculated from the clock in and clock out times on the sorted transaction file. The hourly rate of pay is found on the old master file so that gross pay can be calculated. Tax details on the old master file are used to calculate deductions from the gross pay to arrive at net pay. The cumulative totals on the master file are **amended** (updated); e.g. the tax paid will be added to the total tax paid this year, and a **new master file record** is created.

- **Backups** of files are automatically generated so that corresponding copies of the sorted transaction files and old master files can be used to restore the current files. The ancestral backup system can be used to provide three levels of backup.

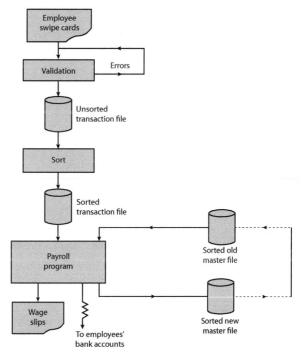

Figure 12.1 *An ICT system for payroll processing*

- Payroll is a **batch** processing system because:
  - All the data to be processed is available before processing begins.
  - There is no need to process the data immediately.
  - The system can be run **off line**.

Airline booking system

A large airline uses an ICT system to store details of flight schedules and passenger bookings.

- The airline's mainframe computer supports **multi-access** as a large number of travel agents want to make enquiries at the same time. The flight information and booking file is direct access for high-speed data retrieval so that the information requested can be kept up to date and displayed instantaneously.

- When the flight information and booking file is being accessed, to avoid double booking, all other attempts to book a seat must be locked out. Once a seat has been booked the flight information and booking file must be updated immediately so that further enquiries show the seat is booked.

- The ICT system is online 24 hours a day and must not be out of action at any time. This is avoided by having two identical computers: the main one in use and an additional computer available as a **hot standby** to use if the main computer breaks down.

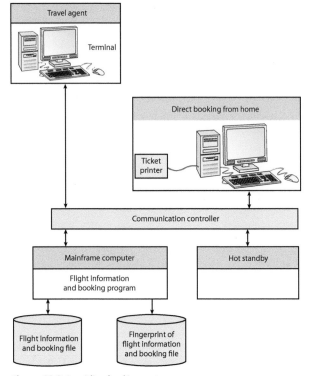

Figure 12.2 *An airline booking system*

- Data **backup** is provided by having two hard disks with the flight information and booking file saved on both of them. Any changes made to one file are made to the other at the same time. This ensures the file is available if one disk becomes faulty. This technique is known as **disk mirroring.**

- An online booking system is a **real-time** processing system because the data input must be processed before any further input and the output will influence further input.

Supermarket stock control

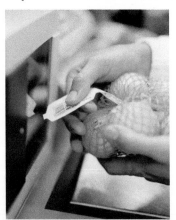

- Supermarkets use **general purpose** ICT systems for a range of applications, including **stock control**. Checkouts or **point of sale (POS)** terminals are connected to the supermarket's main computer and there are terminals in the warehouse and elsewhere.

- Checkouts have a laser scanner which reads the **bar code**. If the bar code cannot be read, the number under the bar code can be entered manually. The bar code contains the product code, which is sent to the main computer where it is used to find the corresponding record in the product information file.

> **TOP TIP**
> The name of a product and its price are *not* stored in the bar code.

Figure 12.3 *A supermarket POS terminal*

- A record on the **product information file** includes the product code to identify the product, the name of the product, the price, the quantity in stock and the reorder level. The name of the product and its price are sent from the main computer to the POS terminal and printed on the customer's receipt.

- The sales made at each checkout are recorded in the product information file as the goods are sold and stock levels go down. Those goods that have a lower number in stock than their reorder level may need to be reordered. The supplier is contacted and requested to send more of them. The ICT system may do this automatically.

- As goods arrive at the supermarket's warehouse, the quantity delivered is entered at a terminal and added to the product information file. If a maximum stock level is set for each product then the quantity reordered can be adjusted so that this level is not exceeded when new supplies arrive at the warehouse.

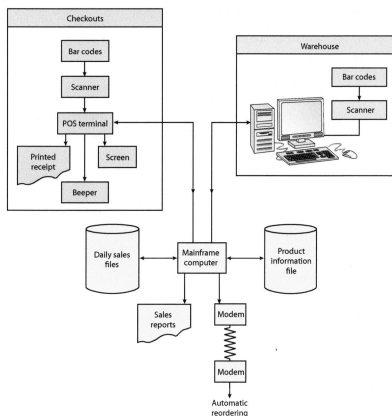

Figure 12.4 *A supermarket stock control system*

Other uses of a stock control system

- Performance of staff can be monitored by checking the number of items sold at each checkout.

- Rate of sales can be used to increase stock of popular goods.

- Pattern of sales can show what needs to be stocked at certain times of the year.

- Extent of theft from the supermarket can be calculated.

Banking

ICT systems are used in banking in:

- **Internet banking** systems

- **automatic teller machines (ATMs)** for cash withdrawals

- **electronic funds transfer (EFT)**, which businesses use to transfer funds from one bank account to another. For example, it is used when customer's pay for goods with their debit or credit card. This process is known as **electronic funds transfer at point of sale (EFTPOS)**.

Figure 12.5 *An ATM*

Figure 12.6 *Paying with a credit card using an EFTPOS machine*

Engineering and manufacturing

- **Computer-aided design (CAD)** software is used to design products, buildings and parts. It provides sets of standard components and basic design elements. Designs can be produced faster and changes to the original design are easier because the full drawing doesn't need to be redone.

- **Computer-aided manufacture (CAM)** is the use of a computer to control manufacture. CAM software generates instructions for the control of **CNC (Computerised Numerical Control)** machines, e.g. computerised lathes for turning and drilling.

- **CAD/CAM** systems combine computer-aided design (CAD) and computer-aided manufacturing (CAM). Engineers use CAD/CAM to create product designs, and then to control the manufacturing process so products are more consistent.

- **Computer-aided engineering (CAE)** systems analyse engineering designs produced by CAD systems, and simulate a variety of conditions to see if the design actually works. CAE features are found in many CAD packages.

- **Process control** is the use of computers to monitor manufacturing processes and to take corrective action to prevent malfunction; for example, ensuring the temperature is at the right level using sensors.

- **Robots** can be used for assembling cars and welding and can perform physical tasks that could be dangerous for humans. Robots can be programmed to do tasks using programming languages or using teach and learn methods, where the robot is physically moved through the actions you want it to do, and the computer converts these into a program, which enables the task to be repeated.

- **Flight simulators** are used to train pilots to fly aircraft, without risk to themselves or to an aircraft. The simulator is mounted on legs, which move when the pilot moves the simulator's controls. The trainee pilot feels the simulator move in the way a real aircraft would move.

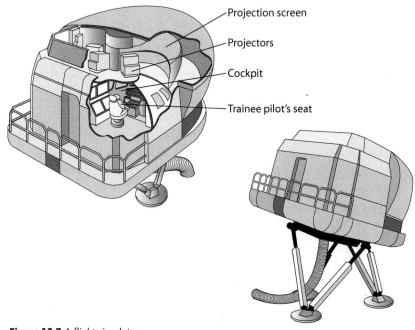

Projection screen

Projectors

Cockpit

Trainee pilot's seat

Figure 12.7 *A flight simulator*

Weather forecasting

Weather forecasts are based on data collected using weather stations, weather balloons and satellites:

- **Weather stations** are groups of sensors that collect information about the current weather. They may have sensors for wind speed and direction, air pressure, temperature and rainfall. The data that is logged is collected on a computer over a network. As well as being used for forecasting, they can also help councils and motorists plan for bad weather conditions.

- **Weather balloons** have a more complex and varied set of instruments than weather stations.

- **Satellites** orbiting the earth allow meteorologists to observe cloud formation throughout the world.

Data from weather stations, weather balloons and satellites are automatically collected and stored. This is an example of **data logging**.

A supercomputer uses mathematical models of the atmosphere to predict what weather conditions will be like in the near future. The models used are constantly being improved and forecasts are increasingly accurate and timely.

Logistics

- Logistics software is used to plan and control the effective delivery and storage of goods and services between the point of origin and the point of consumption in order to meet customer requirements.

Figure 12.8 *A roadside weather station*

- Logistics could involve the organisation of information, transport, materials handling, packaging, stock control, warehousing and security.

Education and libraries

- **Virtual learning environments (VLEs)** help teachers teach and support students' studies by providing learning resources at all times where there is web access. VLEs enable resources to be organised and shared easily, with digital drop boxes to store and submit students' work, access to wikis, blogs and podcasts, and information about grades so progress can be assessed.

- **Computer-assisted learning (CAL)** software helps students learn. CAL provides immediate feedback; enables students to recognise their weaknesses and improve; displays encouraging messages; and can be accessed using a VLE. **Drill and practice** programs help students consolidate learning. **Tutorial** software introduces and teaches new material to students. **Simulations** model real-life situations so the software can be used in the classroom without risk or wastage.

- **School information and management systems (SIMS)** are widely used to help with the day-to-day running of schools. They can produce class lists, create timetables, provide automatic reporting, improve communications quality, provide fast access to information and produce statistics and accounting information automatically.

- **Libraries** use ICT systems to: keep records of books that have been borrowed; provide online searchable catalogues; provide access to electronic books; keep records of borrowers; and send reminders to borrowers who have not returned books.

Law enforcement

- The **police** use ICT systems to help fight crime. National databases help the police identify offenders.

- Other uses of ICT by the police include: managing cases and preparing reports; analysing statistics; tracking criminals who have been tagged; developing contacts with police worldwide; profiling of potential criminals; and accessing information remotely through wireless network links on police cars.

- **Law firms** use ICT to create legal document templates, find information about past judgements, and obtain information about legislation in other countries.

Healthcare and medicine

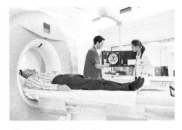

Figure 12.9 *An MRI scan*

- **Computerised patient records** contain notes from all the doctors and institutions that a patient has attended. These are available wherever a patient is being treated. Research based on these records can lead to improved treatments for everyone.

- **Patient monitoring** systems continuously monitor very ill patients. Sensors connected to a computer record vital signs, such as heart rate, and sound an alarm if there are problems.

- **Magnetic resonance imaging (MRI)** and **computer axial tomography (CAT)** scanners produce images that can be viewed in 3-D.

- Medical **expert systems** analyse questions input by a practitioner and provide decision-making support and suggest alternative diagnosis or treatment.

- Using **telemedicine**, patients can visit a doctor online and doctors can treat their patients at a distance.

Entertainment and leisure

- The Internet can be used to **communicate** with friends and family with webcams and video calls.

- **Computer games** of all genres provide entertainment and can be used on a PC or on a games console.

- Using **media streaming**, you can listen to music, watch TV and watch videos on desktop PCs and mobile devices.

- **Personal performance** during sport can be monitored by mobile devices using satellite navigation, and recorded for later analysis.

Social impact

The widespread use of ICT has a significant impact on society, e.g. there is a **digital divide** because some people have easy access to ICT while others do not.

Employment

Employment opportunities have changed:

- There are **fewer unskilled jobs**, e.g. assembly lines with robots now assemble cars.

- **The skills needed for some jobs have changed**, e.g. administrators previously used typewriters but now use word processors. Workers in almost every industry at almost every level have experienced changes in skill requirements.

- **Jobs have been created** in the ICT industry, e.g. in programming, website design and manufacturing, and jobs have been created indirectly, e.g. in video production.

- **How people do their jobs** has changed, e.g. a teacher can have an entire class work through resources on a VLE and provide much less input during the lesson, although considerably more planning and preparation may be needed beforehand.

- **Teleworking** is more common. Instead of going to the office, teleworkers can work from home and communicate with the office online. They avoid the expense and time of commuting. However, teleworkers can miss social interaction with colleagues, and being at home can be distracting. There is a lack of access to the specialist facilities and advice available at work. Companies can employ teleworkers who live a long way away, even in another country. Less floor space is needed at the office, and there is reduced absence because telecommuters can work when the weather prevents travel. However, managers may feel they do not have sufficient control over what workers are doing during working hours and workers may not be available when the company tries to contact them.

- Companies have improved global communications, both within their own organisations and with other companies, to facilitate international trade. The use of online communication tools has minimised the need for employees to travel overseas.

Employees' health can be affected by intense and prolonged computer use. Possible problems are:

- Repetitive strain injury (RSI), e.g. from using a keyboard.

- Fatigue, headaches, and eye problems.

- Backache and similar problems through sitting in an inappropriate posture.

- Trip hazards due to trailing cables.

- Injury from electric shock.

These issues can also affect those who use computers for leisure purposes.

Ergonomics helps reduce health problems and injuries, and includes the following design and arrangement of seating and equipment:

- The operator's chair should have an adjustable height and backrest.

- Monitors should be positioned to avoid daylight reflection and interior lights should be shaded.

- Larger monitor screens should be used.

- Foot and wrist supports should be available.

To prevent trip hazards and electric shocks due to trailing cables, cabling should be in trunking or out of reach. RCDs (residual current devices) should also be used. These are designed to turn off the power if the user receives an electric shock. Rules governing the user's behaviour also reduce the risk of health problems and injuries. This includes taking regular breaks and having regular eye examinations.

Privacy

Privacy refers to the right of individuals to determine what information is stored about them and how that information is used. Problems arise because businesses, organisations and governments hold personal information which is easily copied and transmitted across international networks.

Different countries have different regulations. In the UK, the **Data Protection Acts** (1984 and 1998) set out principles for handling personal information. Data must be:

- Fairly and lawfully processed in line with subjects' rights.

- Used only for its intended purpose and not kept for longer than necessary.

- Adequate for its intended purpose, relevant to it and not excessive.

- Accurate, that is: up-to-date and complete.

- Stored securely so unauthorised people do not have access to it.

- Not transferred to countries that do not have similar laws to protect personal privacy.

Computer crime

Computer crime is possible because of the widespread use of ICT. Such crime would not exist if ICT systems were not used and could not be exploited for financial gain. It includes:

- **Software piracy** which is the copying, downloading, use or sale of software without an appropriate license.

- **Copyright violation** which occurs when, e.g. music or pictures, are copied or downloaded without an appropriate licence.

- Criminal **hackers** who gain unauthorised access to an ICT system in order to steal, alter or destroy data, e.g. they might steal money by transferring it from one bank account to another. Ethical hackers are employed by an organisation to attempt to gain access to an organisation's ICT systems in order to alert them to vulnerabilities that can be exploited by criminal hackers.

- **Identity theft** where someone pretends to be you in order to commit fraud, e.g. buy goods in your name.

- **Phishing** attacks involve sending unsolicited emails inviting you to a response which involves entering your username, password and other personal details, e.g. you receive an email which seems to be from your bank asking you to use a hyperlink in the email to access your bank account. You click on the link and are directed to a fake website and are asked to enter your bank account details. Criminals use these details to steal money from your bank account. To avoid this type of scam, do not use the link in the email.

Security

Security is important in ensuring privacy, data integrity and preventing computer crime.

Physical safeguards include:

- **Access control** to ICT rooms, e.g. use of swipe cards or biometrics.

- **Access monitoring**, e.g. use of CCTV cameras.

- **Data security:** e.g. storage of backups in a fireproof safe in another location.

- **Protection from fire, floods, theft and malicious damage:** use buildings and areas where problems are reduced, e.g. servers housed in a concrete underground bunker on top of a hill that is accessible only through a well-guarded and narrow passage. Individual computers should be clamped to desks; have burglar alarms in addition to those for the building; and CCTV surveillance.

- **Contingency plans** and **disaster recovery** arrangements so that recovery is swift and ICT systems continue operating with a minimum of disruption, e.g. make sure you can run your ICT systems elsewhere if your own equipment is out of action.

Software safeguards include:

- **File access rights** which allow access to particular files to those people who need it and block others.

- **Transaction logs** which track alterations to ICT systems and record who accessed the data.

- **Data security:** e.g. regular backups.

See Chapter 9 for software safeguards that prevent threats from the Internet.

Figure 12.10 *A popular virus scanner*

Individual responsibility

How individuals use the Internet has considerable social impact. Behave sensibly to protect yourself and others, as the openness and freedom of the Internet can be abused. You should:

- Keep usernames and passwords secret. Do not write them down.
- Change passwords regularly.
- Only share your personal data (e.g. your name, age or telephone number) with people you trust.
- Not publish anyone else's personal data unless you have their permission.
- Make sure you know who stores your personal data and that it is correct.
- Not copy someone else's work without acknowledging them; this is plagiarism.
- Not download software or music unless it is copyright free or you have a licence.
- Not attempt to hack ICT systems. Hacking is an illegal activity in many countries.
- Not believe everything you see or hear online.
- Use virus scanners and other malware detection software. This protects you from others and keeps the Web safe for everyone.
- Be polite and reasonable. If you feel you are the victim of cyber bullying seek help. Don't bully others.
- Use secure wireless networks wherever possible.

Worked Example

Virtual learning environments (VLEs) are widely used in education.

a) State two advantages of a VLE for a student.

b) State two advantages of a VLE for a teacher.

c) Give two reasons why a teacher may prefer not to use a VLE in the classroom.

TOP TIP

Make sure you discuss both advantages AND disadvantages if the question asks you to do so.

Answers

a) For students, there are many advantages of using a VLE. Two of these are:

Students can access learning resources on the VLE at any time, at home or at school.

Students can view their grade profile so they can see the progress they are making.

b) For teachers, there are many advantages of using a VLE. Two of these are:

Learning resources are more organised and are more easily shared.

Students' work submitted online can be marked and feedback given online.

c) Teachers may prefer not to use a VLE in the classroom because e.g.:

There is not always adequate network access.

Some activities do not require electronic resources, e.g. sport.

1. Which security precaution would help protect you from a virus attached to an email?

    A username and password

    B file access rights

    C virus scanner

    D transaction log   *(1 mark)*

2. Which technology is used when you pay for goods at a checkout using a credit card?

    A VLE

    B CAD/CAM

    C EFTPOS

    D ATM   *(1 mark)*

3. An international airline stores flight booking information. What type of computer would be used to store this information?

    A PC

    B mainframe

    C tablet

    D laptop   *(1 mark)*

4. Customers of an online bank cannot do all their banking online. Which task could NOT be done online?

    A Deposit cash

    B Look at a statement

    C Transfer money between accounts

    D Open a new account   *(1 mark)*

5. What should you do to help keep your password secure?

    A Tell your best friend

    B Keep it secret

    C Use your first name

    D Write it down   *(1 mark)*

6. What information is stored in a bar code?

    A The price

    B The product code

    C The description

    D The number of the checkout   *(1 mark)*

7. ICT has had an impact on individuals and society.

    a) Describe the impact of ICT on people at home.
        (2 marks)

    b) Describe the impact of ICT on education.
        (2 marks)

    c) Describe the impact of ICT on people at work.
        (2 marks)

TOP TIP

Describe what ICT has made possible that was not previously possible.

8. Lesley works on a checkout at a large supermarket.

    a) Describe how Lesley inputs data to the supermarket's stock control system.   *(1 mark)*

    b) What type of application software does the supermarket use for stock control?   *(1 mark)*

    c) A customer is given an itemised receipt with a brief description of each item they have bought and its price. Describe the process that makes this possible.   *(4 marks)*

    d) The supermarket manager asks Lesley to scan customers' shopping more quickly. Describe how the supermarket manager knows the speed Lesley works, and why Lesley might be concerned about this.   *(2 marks)*

    e) The supermarket automatically reorders cans of baked beans from the supplier. Describe the process that makes this possible.   *(4 marks)*

    f) The stock control system tells the manager that sales of ice cream are higher than usual. Describe how the manager could respond to this.   *(1 mark)*

Preparation for the examinations

How the qualification is assessed

The Edexcel International GCSE in ICT is made up of two papers, each contributing 50% to your overall mark, and examined in the English language. The papers cover three assessment objectives, and the content of the qualification is defined by learning outcomes. For further details about the qualification, see the specification and assessment materials on the Edexcel website (www.edexcel.com).

Assessment objectives

Here is a table summarising the assessment objectives and their weightings in the examination:

AO1: Knowledge and understanding Students should be able to: • demonstrate knowledge and understanding of the specification content.	20–40%
AO2: Application Students should be able to: • apply their knowledge, skills and understanding of ICT to a range of situations to solve problems.	40–60%
AO3: Evaluation Students should be able to: • reflect critically on the way they and others use, create or develop ICT systems; • discuss and review the impact of ICT applications in the wider world.	20–30%

Paper 1

Paper 1 is a written examination which is 1 hour and 30 minutes in length and students must complete all questions. It is in two sections: in Section A, students answer multiple-choice questions or similar, and in section B students are required to give short written responses. There is space below each question for you to write your answer and the marks that can be awarded for each question are printed on the examination paper. The total number of marks for this paper is 100.

Paper 2

Paper 2 is a practical paper which is 3 hours long and there is no choice of questions. You carry out practical tasks based on a scenario described at the start of the paper. You can use any hardware, operating system or application software to do the tasks. You print your work for assessment. The total number of marks for this paper is 100.

Learning outcomes

The learning outcomes are divided into five areas: ICT systems, Impact of ICT, Use ICT Systems, Find and Select Information, and Develop, Present and Communicate Information. You can find in the introduction to this revision guide which learning objectives are covered in each chapter. Paper 1 covers all of these areas. In Paper 2, the content you will be assessed on is Use ICT Systems, Find and Select Information, and Develop, Present and Communicate Information.

Before the examination

- **Pack your bag the night before** the examination, and make sure you have all the equipment you will need in the examination. This may not be available to borrow and could limit your success.

- **Get a good night's sleep.** It's important to be fully rested before the exam, so don't stay up late revising.

- **Make sure you eat properly.** Get up early and have a good breakfast to prepare yourself for the examination.

- **Go to the lavatory** just before the examination. Your time is wasted if you have to go during the examination.

- **Arrive in good time**. Make sure that you arrive at the examination centre early. If you are late you will not be allowed extra time.

During the examination

- In the examination, **start as soon as possible**.

- **Read the instructions** and do what you are asked.

- **Attempt all the questions.** Correct answers are awarded marks. Marks are not taken off for incorrect answers except in multiple choice questions if you select too many options.

- **Allow enough time** to answer every question. Work out how much time you can spend on each mark, and use this as a guide to how much time to spend on each question.

- **Read the question thoroughly**. You will only be awarded marks for a correct answer to the actual question set.

- Always give **as much detail as possible** in the space provided. If it is helpful, give examples and draw diagrams.

- Each point you make should be **quite different**. If there are three marks for a question, make at least three different points.

- **Avoid vague answers**, e.g. if you give answers such as 'quicker' or 'cheaper', you are unlikely to be awarded marks unless you say, e.g. quicker than what, or why it is quicker.

- **Give examples**, as these can help make a vague answer much clearer.

- **To describe the difference** between two methods, e.g. using a keyboard and an Optical Mark Reader for input, make a clear statement for each. For example, 'inputting data by typing it on a keyboard takes much longer than reading an OMR form that has been filled incorrectly'.

- **Write legibly**. If examiners cannot read your work they cannot award marks for it.

- Use **correct spelling, punctuation and grammar**. Spell ICT technical words accurately.

- When using software, **change the default settings** so it is clear you can use the features of the software, e.g. if the default font is Times New Roman then change it to Calibri.

- Examiners expect A* students to answer **correctly** and **in full** questions that other students get wrong.

- **Don't leave before the end**. Spend all the time answering questions or checking your answers.

Vocabulary used in examinations

You need to know what examiners mean when they set questions so that you can provide them with the right answer. The table below explains words used in the examination papers.

Command word	Meaning
CREATE	Open a new item, e.g. create a file.
CROSS	Place a cross in a box.
DESCRIBE	Write a short account of what is done or observed, e.g. the advantages of a wireless network.
DISCUSS	Write at greater length about similarities and differences, and advantages and disadvantages of two or more methods or items, e.g. discuss the advantages and disadvantages of wireless and wired networks.
DISPLAY	Show on the monitor screen.
EXPLAIN	Write an account of why or how something is done, giving reasons, e.g. explain what is meant by 'copyright'.
GIVE	Write a short answer, perhaps a single word or a short sentence, e.g. give two advantages.
IDENTIFY	Give sufficient information so that it is clear what is meant, e.g. identify two risks when a computer is connected to the Internet.
NAME	Write down the name, e.g. of an item of hardware.
PRODUCE	Make, e.g. produce a report.
STATE	Write a sentence, e.g. state what is meant by RAM.
TAKE	Make, e.g. take a screen shot.
TICK	Place a tick in a box.
WORK THROUGH	Start at the beginning and do each task one after the other.

Glossary

Absolute cell reference   A spreadsheet cell reference that remains unchanged when moved or copied to another cell, e.g. in Excel, $A$7.

Ancestral file system   A way of organising file backups. In its simplest form, it consists of the son (the latest copy), the father (the previous copy) and the grandfather (the copy before the previous copy), each with the data that was used to update it. These copies are kept in increasingly secure locations.

Application software   Software designed to do a specific job, e.g. a word processor.

ATM (Automated Teller Machine)   A specialised computer terminal that provides access to banking transactions. Often called a cashpoint or 'hole in the wall'.

Backing storage   A means of saving programs and data outside the computer's RAM memory, e.g. hard disk.

Backup   A backup of a file is another copy of it. The ancestral file system is often used.

Barcode   A code represented by a series of vertical black and white lines, often used to encode an identity number.

Baud   A measure of the transmission speed of a network. One baud is one bit per second.

Bitmap   Graphics formed by a pattern of dots or pixels, e.g. .bmp files.

Broadband   Data transmission using ADSL (asymmetric digital subscriber line) over telephone lines or cable.

Browser   Client software used to browse the Web, e.g. Google Chrome.

CAD (Computer-Aided Design)   CAD is used to produce 2D and 3D designs.

CAI (Computer-Aided Instruction) or CAL (Computer-Assisted Learning)   Using a computer to help learn a particular subject or skill, e.g. in Mathematics, using software to practise multiplication tables.

CAM (Computer-Aided Manufacture)   Using a computer to control the manufacture of a product.

Cell   The intersection of a row and a column in a spreadsheet.

Cell range reference   Referring to a rectangular block of cells in a spreadsheet by giving the cell reference of the top left-hand and the bottom right-hand cells; e.g. **A4:G10.**

Character   Characters include A to Z, 0 to 9, and punctuation marks.

Chat   Communicating interactively in real time over the Internet.

Client/server   A network with clients and at least one server.

Clip art   Pictures that can be imported into a word processor or other software.

Create   Set up for the first time.

Crop   To remove that part of an image outside the selected area.

Cursor   The symbol on your screen that follows the movement of your mouse, e.g. a pointer.

Cursor control keys   The arrow keys on a keyboard used to control the movement of the cursor.

Data capture   The collection of data for input to a computer. Data capture can be online (e.g. point of sale terminals at supermarket checkouts) or offline (e.g. questionnaires).

Data logging   The use of sensors to measure and record environmental conditions, e.g. in a weather station.

Database   A means of storing and accessing information. The information is structured by subdividing it into tables, rows (records) and columns (fields).

DDE (Direct Data Entry)   Data entry directly to the program that is processing the data, e.g. using bar code readers.

Dialog box   An application window offering advice or information and asking for a response.

Directory   A collection of files and subdirectories organised in a hierarchical tree structure. Also known as a folder.

Disk mirroring   A backup method where data is written simultaneously to two hard disks. If one disk fails, the other is available.

Documentation   A written description of how to install the software on a computer, what it does and how it is used, e.g. help files.

Download   Transfer a file from a web server to your computer over the Internet.

Dynaset   A group of records produced as a result of a database query.

EFT (Electronic Funds Transfer)   A method of transferring money between bank accounts using a network.

EFTPOS   EFT at Point Of Sale, e.g. a supermarket checkout.

Email client   The email software on a computer in a client/server network.

Email server   The file server that manages, distributes and stores email.

Encryption   Encoding (scrambling) data during storage or transmission so that it cannot be understood by someone who does not have the encryption key.

Field   A data item within a record, i.e. a column in a database table.

File server   A computer attached to a network whose main function is to enable PCs to access shared files stored on hard disk.

Firewall   Software used to prevent unauthorised users gaining access to a computer from the Internet.

Folder   A directory.

Font   A complete set of consistently shaped characters, e.g. Arial. Also called typeface.

FTP (File Transmission Protocol)   A set of rules for **downloading** and **uploading** files from servers via the Internet.

Gigabyte (GB)   1024 Megabytes or 2^{30} bytes.

Graphics   Pictures, images or symbols that can be processed by a computer.

GUI (Graphical User Interface)   A visual user interface that uses windows, menus, icons and pointers.

Hacker   An unauthorised user of a computer system who has broken into the system. Hacking is an illegal activity.

Hardware   The physical components of a computer system, e.g. a monitor.

Help   Instructions describing how to use a piece of software, e.g. online help.

HTML (Hypertext Markup Language)   A language used to create web pages.

Hyperlink   A link in a web page or other document which when clicked takes the user to another web page or document.

ICT system   The organisation of human and other resources, including ICT, into a coherent system for the purposeful processing of information.

Interactive processing   When a user and a computer are in active two-way communication.

Internet   A global network that consists of a collection of smaller interconnected networks. There is no central organisation or ownership.

Intranet   A version of the Internet accessible only within a company or organisation.

IP address   The unique address that identifies a computer on the Internet.

ISP (Internet Service Provider)   A company that is directly connected to the Internet and gives you access to it, usually for a fee.

Kilobyte (KB)   1024 or 2^{10} bytes.

Key field (or primary key)   Every record in a database table should have a unique key field that identifies the record.

LAN (Local Area Network)   A network in a building, department or school.

Laptop   A portable computer that is small enough and light enough to be carried around.

Open (or Load)   To retrieve from backing storage.

Mail merge   The merging of a data file and a standard letter to produce personalised mail.

Master file   A data file that is used to store most of the data for a particular application. It is updated by a transaction file.

Megabyte (MB)   1024 kilobytes or 2^{20} bytes.

Merge   To combine two or more items into a single item.

MICR (Magnetic Ink Character Recognition)   A method of input where characters printed in magnetic ink are read directly into a computer. Used to process cheques.

MIS (Management Information System)   A comprehensive, integrated ICT system for management and administration.

Multitasking   When one user, on one computer, is apparently running more than one program at the same time.

Narrowband   Narrowband is data transmission over a telephone line at speeds up to 56 Kbps.

Network   A network is a system of interconnected computers, e.g. LANs.

NIC (Network Interface Card) A card that is installed in a computer to enable it to communicate with a network.

Non-volatile ROM memory is non-volatile; that is, its contents are permanent. They are retained when the computer is switched off. Information stored on backing storage is also non-volatile.

Notebook A smaller version of a laptop computer. Usually A4 size.

OCR (Optical Character Recognition) The use of software and a scanner to recognise printed or written characters.

OMR (Optical Mark Recognition) An input method where pencil marks on paper are detected. The position of the mark is interpreted as information. Used for UK National Lottery numbers.

Online Connected to the network and in communication with it.

Open (or Load) To retrieve from backing storage.

Operating system An OS is software that controls and monitors the resources of a computer and acts as an interface between the user and the computer, e.g. Microsoft Windows.

Peer-to-peer A network in which each computer can communicate directly with every other computer attached to the network.

Peripheral A peripheral is a hardware device that is connected to a computer system but is not a part of the computer itself, e.g. a printer.

Phishing Phishing is done by sending a fraudulent email that pretends to be from a reliable source, e.g. a bank. The email asks you to enter personal information, e.g. usernames and passwords. These are used for identity theft and fraud.

POS (Point Of Sale) terminal For example, a supermarket checkout.

Primary key A key field in a database table that uniquely identifies a record.

Process control The use of computers to monitor manufacturing processes and take corrective action if these become destabilised. Used in chemical plants and oil refineries.

Program A set of instructions used to control the operation of a computer.

Protocol A set of rules and procedures, e.g. to control the transmission and reception of data so that different devices can communicate with each other.

Proxy Server A proxy server regulates data communication between a client on a LAN and a web server, speeding up web access, and acting as a firewall or filter protecting the LAN.

Query A method of searching for information in a database.

RAM (Random Access Memory) RAM is volatile read/write memory used to store programs while they are being executed and data while it is being processed.

Real-time processing The processing of data being input which takes place so fast that when more data is input the results of the processing are already available. Real-time processing occurs in real time, i.e. as it happens.

Record A record is a collection of related fields about a specific subject, e.g. a row in a database table.

Relative cell reference A reference to a cell in a spreadsheet that changes with respect to its current position when moved or copied; for example, A5.

ROM (Read-Only Memory) Memory within a computer that can only be read. ROM is non-volatile.

Root The top directory in a file system that is organised as a hierarchical tree.

Router Specialised hardware that receives data and redirects it between networks, e.g. between a home network and the Internet.

Search engine A website that enables you to find information on the Web by typing in keywords or phrases.

Sensor An input device that measures physical quantities such as temperature and humidity.

Server On a network, a computer running software that allows resources to be shared with the other computers (called **clients**).

Smart card A card similar in shape and size to a credit card but with an embedded microprocessor and storage capacity.

Smart phone A mobile phone capable of web browsing and email, with a calendar and address book, camera and capable of running applications.

Software Computer programs.

Software piracy The unauthorised copying, use or sale of software that is copyrighted.

Speech recognition Input to a computer by speaking words to it.

Speech synthesis   Sounds generated by a computer that synthesise human speech.

Standalone   A computer that is not connected to any other computer.

Surfing   Browsing through information on web servers by wandering from page to page by selecting hyperlinks.

Swipe card   A card, usually the size of a credit card that is swiped through an input device. It usually has a magnetic stripe on it that stores data, e.g. a loyalty card.

System unit   The cabinet containing the CPU, the hard disk and some other components of a computer. Peripheral devices are attached to the system unit.

Table   A list of information in a database shown in rows and columns. A database file may have several tables within it.

Tablet   A tablet computer has the functions of a laptop built into a case similar to a large smart phone.

TCP/IP   Transmission Control Protocol/Internet Protocol. A set of protocols used during the transfer of data from one computer to another over the Internet.

Transaction file   A file used to store recent data captured since the last master file update. The transaction file is used to update the master file.

Update   To bring a file or document up to date by amending, editing, inserting or deleting data.

Upload   Transfer a file from your computer to a web server over the Internet.

URL (Uniform Resource Locator)   The address of a web server; e.g. the URL for the University of Huddersfield is **http://www.hud.ac.uk.**

User-friendly   Easy for users to operate and understand.

User interface   The way in which a computer system communicates with users, e.g. graphical user interface (GUI) such as Windows.

Validation   A check that data is sensible, e.g. a range check.

Verification   A check on the accuracy of input, i.e. a check that what is written on a source document is accurately transferred to the computer.

Virus   A virus is a computer program that infects a computer system, usually without the user's knowledge. Viruses may be benign but more often they cause damage.

Voice recognition   The identification of a person by recognising their voice.

Voice synthesis   The ability of a computer to produce sounds resembling human speech.

Volatile memory   Volatile memory loses its contents when the power is switched off. RAM memory is volatile.

WAN (Wide Area Network)   A network spread over a wide area, possibly international, making use of cable, wireless and satellite communications.

World Wide Web (or just Web)   A multimedia information service accessible over the Internet.

Website   A server connected to the Internet used to store web pages.

Wireless access point   A device that communicates with wireless Network Interface Cards (NICs) in computers, allowing them to connect to a network.

Index

Index